Say His Name

A Mother's Grief

Susan Glynn Robinson

Peacock Press

Hockessin, Delaware

First published 2020 by Peacock Press
www.SusanRobinsonAuthor.com
Printed in the U.S.A.

10 9 8 7 6 5 4 3 2 1

ISBN 978-1-7335067-6-2

Cover design by Ezequiel Decarli

To Collin

Until someday.

I know you won't like
that this book includes so much sorrow and despair,
so here's a chuckle just for you.

Linus: After you've died, do you get to come back?
Charlie Brown: If they stamp your hand.
—Charles M. Schulz

Table of Contents

Acknowledgments

Resources

About the Author

Preface

This is not the book I always dreamed of writing. But it's the one I needed to write, and the one bereaved parents need to read.

On March 30, 1998, my sixteen-year-old son Collin died. My spirit followed into the ether, and like a scene from *Invasion of the Body Snatchers*, Grief took over my body, heart, and mind. Though a strong woman from a line of strong women, I became codependent, alternately hating and loving this abuser. Grief chewed at me like a cancer while it cradled me within memory. I begged for Superman to fly backward around the earth and reset time. I sobbed; screamed; withdrew. Nothing had prepared me for such intense emotion, the evisceration of my sense of control and faith, or the tenacity of incapacitation and despair. Still, I clung to this monster on my back. Ours had become a symbiotic bond—a visceral link to Collin.

Few people understood. To them, Grief was something to be packed away—the sooner, the better—or at least medicated or distracted into submission. No one wants to feel uncomfortable, and Grief—no cordial companion—made them squirm.

Books and support groups set up healing and acceptance as short-term goals. People bragged about getting on with their lives or how their children's deaths had spurred them to noble accomplishments—or that their child's death had meaning. Pop some Prozac, they urged, go back to work, and things will be back to normal (a "new normal," they admitted) in a few years. I think of it as more of a "new abnormal." And of course I should do this on my own, behind closed doors, because Grief makes others uncomfortable.

No one seemed to view mourning as necessary or constructive. It was an obstacle to overcome, a hurdle to leap over and never look back.

I tried to follow those rules, but my heart had its own mind. Determined—defiant—to grieve in its own way and in its own time, it fought my attempts to circumvent it, parrying with fatigue, cloudy vision, agoraphobia, and despair.

As I researched mourning rituals of earlier eras and cultures, I discovered my immersion in grief was not abnormal. The problem was modern western society's revulsion for mourning.

Like an iceberg, 90% of grief hides beneath the surface. *Say His Name: A Mother's Grief* is my exposé of grief, revealing the distress most hide to shield the fear they are the only ones so anguished. They may also hide their grief to avoid hurting others. Grief is personal, but should be neither solitary nor secret. If we permitted ourselves and others to mourn openly and communally, the newly-bereaved would know what to expect, and friends and loved ones could provide much-needed support rather than withholding it from a misplaced respect for privacy.

When my grief was new, books by other bereaved parents helped me know what to expect. If you are a power griever, as I am, I hope to reassure you that you are not alone and need not be "over it" just because others tire of the drama. If you are a speed griever, know that this, too, is a valid reaction to death, but that not everyone is able or wants to mourn the way you do. There is no "correct" way to grieve. Those who deal with it quickly get all the kudos: "I'm glad to see you smile again!" and "It's so good that you're back at the gym!" The extended grievers, not so much: "Please smile, just for me?" "It would do you good to get back to the gym!" Whatever you need to do to salve your soul and protect your heart is right.

This book also offers hope to those who support the bereaved. If someone you love is grieving, insight into the iceberg's hidden parts will help you to better understand and empathize. May this knowledge also make you better able to deal with Grief should it ever become your shadow.

Although it is for others, writing this book has helped me in my grief work, and I am pleased that it honors my son. A work of community, it began in 2002 as my master's thesis. My instructors introduced me to authors whose writing helped me find an authentic voice and personal style in which to share it.

It was through Annie Dillard's *The Writing Life* that I first found metaphor meaningful— saw it as more than just flowery passages to skip over to get back to the plot. Dillard can put an entire paragraph into a single phrase: "You were made and set here to give voice to this, your own astonishment." Whereas literal prose asks literal interpretation, Dillard's poetic inferences invite musing about deeper insights and multiple levels of meaning.

Similarly, surgeon-cum-writer Richard Selzer's figurative style reveals passion—and compassion—in ways straightforward narrative never approaches. And any author who makes you shake your head and say, "Wow, I never thought of that!" on every other page not only provides a delightful read but facilitates personal growth. Emitting sparks such as "If Pythagoras is right, there is no silence in the universe. Even the stars make music as they move," Selzer is that kind of genius. In this book, I have aspired to the poetic voices of these authors.

Another "Wow, I never thought of that!" author who informs my work is Joan Borysenko, a former cancer cell researcher whose writing is shot through with both clear insight into feminine biology and psychology and deep, unapologetic, non-evangelical, and—I know this sounds like an oxymoron—down-to-earth mysticism. In the depths of my despair, many writers (and friends) wagged scolding fingers as magic wands to turn my doubt into faith. Some offered to share their faith with me, even though faith isn't something you can gift someone—it's something that must develop organically. Borysenko challenged me to look at faith holistically, as a concept: "Grace is a paradox; apparently wonderful events can curb our growth, while devastating events may spur it."

Perhaps my own questions about life and death attracted me to possibilities raised by the intermingling of spirituality and science. Thanatologist Elisabeth Kübler-Ross's emotional involvement with the subjects of her research on death and dying and her theory about the stages of grief provided the original structure for my thesis. I reconsidered my approach after other researchers questioned the validity of stages of grief.[1] However, my experience roughly followed the stages.

A Broken Heart Still Beats After Your Child Dies by Anne McCracken and Mary Semel, a compilation of writings by famous authors about loss, showed me that my grief monster had lived dozens of previous lives and that many of its hosts reacted as I had. It affected me so profoundly I read nearly the whole book through a lens of tears. My attempts to describe my grief were often met with blank stares, and here was an entire book about grief by the best wordsmiths who ever lived! Shocked, I discovered that Robert Frost lost four children, Percy and Mary Shelley three children, and Mark Twain lost a wife and two daughters.

In "The Death of Jean," Twain viewed his daughter's death through his dog's eyes in an account simple yet excruciating:

> They told me the first mourner to come was the dog. He came uninvited, and stood up on his hind legs and rested his forepaws upon the trestle, and took a last long look at the face that was so dear to him, then went his way as silently as he had come. He knows.

I now understood it was because William Shakespeare's own son died at age eleven that he could evoke such empathy in lines like these from *King John:*

> Grief fills the room up of my absent child,
> Lies in his bed, walks up and down with me,
> Puts on his pretty looks, repeats his words,
> Remembers me of all his gracious parts,
> Stuffs out his vacant garments with his form;
> Then have I reason to be fond of grief.

---

1 Michael Shermer, "Five Fallacies of Grief: Debunking Psychological Stages," *Scientific American* (Nov. 1, 2008). Retrieved from https://www.scientificamerican.com/article/five-fallacies-of-grief/ on September 21, 2020.

Besides the impression these authors' accounts made on me, I was stirred by the essays written by one of the book's editors, Mary Semel. Her words could have been mine:

> The same thoughts revolve over and over. How can it be? How can my lively sixteen-year-old son be gone forever? It makes no sense that this life which I cared for with all my heart and soul was wiped out in one cataclysmic moment. What makes life? Where did it go? What can I do to bring it back? There must be something.

Victor Hugo, Herman Melville, Fyodor Dostoevsky, W.E.B. duBois, William Faulkner, William Wordsworth, and Patricia Neal and Roald Dahl are among the dozens of other authors included whose words about their children's deaths touched me. I have a new appreciation of *Peter Pan* after learning it was inspired by the death of J. M. Barrie's older brother David. Excerpts in *A Broken Heart Still Beats* also led me to seek out the full versions of works by Anne Morrow Lindbergh, C. S. Lewis, and Barbara Kingsolver. All are adept at the same metaphorical insight as Dillard and Selzer. Kingsolver's use of it in fiction helped me as I wrote in story style the true account of Collin's hospitalization and death.

This creative nonfiction, however, required more than just images and metaphor. I also needed to recount events clearly, directly, and actively, and to let the story speak for itself, rather than explaining every emotion and thought. For that, works by Gay Talese, Tobias Wolff, Ann Beattie, and Raymond Carver served as invaluable examples.

Although I sought out books on writing poetry (because I felt deficient in that area), all the other writing resources came to me serendipitously as I engaged in other pursuits. An observation Joan Borysenko made at an Omega Institute/New Age Publishing conference I attended in 1999 stuck with me.

Borysenko discussed information from her book *A Woman's Book of Life: The Biology, Psychology, and the Spirituality of the Feminine Life Cycle.* She explained that many differences in behavior between men and women are hard-wired into the brain. Men, she said, set precise, well-defined goals and follow a linear sequence of steps to achieve them. Women approach tasks more holistically, taking in information, sometimes unconsciously, from all sides and at different times to form a data mass. From these clues, a decision emerges intuitively about how to proceed. Thus women may appear undirected or unfocused when they are actively involved in preparing and planning for a task.

This is how *Say His Name: A Mother's Grief* evolved for me—less linear planning and more holistic information gathering, distillation of perceptions, and analysis of techniques. From this critical mass, a book emerged. My true story is told through multiple genres—narrative, story, journaling, poetry, essay, satire—because each brings a different perspective. You may find the shifts discomfiting, but they are a purposeful reflection that grief is uncomfortable and grievers' disjointed thoughts veer wildly from one moment to the next. Although my own creative work, it is connected, weblike, to others' ideas. For it is ideas and words that keep us all linked in spirit. It is how Collin and I still hold fast to each other over the chasm of death.

I
Vigil

How did you know
that sleep is just wasted time
there is no good reason to eat broccoli
you couldn't wait to grow up to be an expert
on salamanders
and that experiencing life meant growing it
under your fingernails?

It Begins

My husband and I stood at the entrance to the Neurological Critical Care Unit. Its two large steel doors loomed like the gates to some impenetrable fortress in one of our son's video games. A buzzer and a click sounded as the doors unlocked. Ed's shoulders slumped and he pressed a palm to his eyes as he held the door for me.

"Ed, please," I said, touching his arm. "Let's not grieve for him while he's still alive."

Ed wiped his eyes with his sleeve and nodded. A few strands of gray shone as he combed his fingers through his hair.

We hesitated just a moment, then stepped into the unit. It was larger than I'd expected, a long counter marking the staff area on the right and glass-walled, curtained patient rooms on the left. I wondered how many rooms held teenagers like our Collin.

We stepped around a laundry cart and walked along the curved passage, guided by the room numbers. In one, an elderly man lay in the bed, still. Another was empty. Collin's room would be toward the end. Five . . . six . . . seven. . . . Ed lagged behind. The corridor loomed, endless, the hallway from a horror movie whose end keeps moving farther away.

Ten. The glass door was closed and the curtains pulled. We entered and stopped short. *Oh my God,* I thought. I clutched my husband's sleeve to steady myself. Ed had tried to tell me how bad this was, but I hadn't allowed it to be true.

The scene swam before me, surreal. Collin sat nearly upright in the bed, his eyes closed. His head was wrapped with gauze, his neck encircled with a cervical collar. Paler than usual, his face looked puffy and distorted. A plastic breathing tube protruded from his mouth and was taped to his face. The tube was connected to a large, boxy machine at his right. Next to it loomed an even larger machine, its multicolored wires disappearing under Collin's bandage. He was motionless except for the tidal rise and fall of his chest under the crisp white sheet. A tube snaked out from under the cover and drained liquid gold into a bag that hung on the bedside. Collin's arms lay exposed, a blood pressure cuff encircling his right bicep, IV needles piercing the back of his left hand and the crook of his elbow. The IV tubes coiled to two circular chrome stands hung all around with a dozen bags of fluid—priceless ornaments on gaudy silver Christmas trees. Three machines with blinking red lights and pulsing, jagged lines stood next to them. Except for the machines' soft bleat and Collin's rhythmic breathing, the room was quiet.

I moved to my son's right side and found an opening among the tubes and machines where I could get close to his face. Blood had dried around his nose and in his right ear, and the bandage covered his left ear. He looked strangely placid. I stroked Collin's cheek with the backs of my fingers and kissed him, searching for his scent amid the blood and antiseptic. "Mommy's here," I said.

The scene shouldn't have unnerved me. A fan of the television program *ER*, I even enjoyed watching *The Operation* on TLC. I wasn't one to panic at the sight of blood—the neighborhood kids all came to me to clean up their cuts and scrapes. Upon our arrival to the ER, Ed and I had been ushered to a private "crying room," which screamed *serious.* And I'd had three hours while Collin was in surgery to brace myself for bandages and beeps and IV bags. Dr. B., the neurosurgeon, prepared us for the worst when he slunk from the operating room and stuck his scalpel into my heart. His words are seared there, as surely as if he had flayed open my chest and inscribed them with a red-hot iron.

"We were able to stop the bleeding," he said, not meeting our eyes, "but there is excessive swelling of the brain matter, which has probably caused substantial brain damage. The situation is very grave. I'm sorry I can't give you better news."

Railing at his pessimism and grim bedside manner let me continue to deny the grave nature of Collin's injury—an aneurysm had exploded in his brain. Or maybe my natural optimism made me assume everything would be all right—of course they would fix him. A poster in my classroom at school read, "Nothing is impossible." But the moment I saw Collin, my trusty steel nerves coiled into Slinkys and my entire body buzzed with the adrenaline of terror.

I took Collin's right hand—the only body part free from medical assault—and massaged it. His fingers felt stiff and didn't respond to my touch. Taken aback, it took me a moment to remember—the coma. The doctors had induced coma, as Collin's cranial pressure was 105.

"Normal is zero," the nurse, Tammy, told us. "A bad headache is about ten."

Oh my God.

Collin's stillness was unnatural for the child I'd dubbed "the perpetual motion machine." At a restaurant years ago, after Collin spilled his milk for the third time, I whispered to Ed that we forgot to install an off switch. Now, I winced. This wasn't what I meant. The machines, glowing and pulsing and beeping, seemed more alive.

Tammy rolled a machine aside and pulled two chairs to Collin's bedside. Ed and I sat and stared at our son. I gripped Collin's hand, and Ed laid his hand on Collin's leg. He lifted the sheet. Collin's legs were covered in blue fleece, wraps that maintained circulation. Boots, I had heard them called.

"Look more like leggings," I groused to no one in particular. "Why don't they call them leggings?" I looked at Ed, my eyes pleading. "What are we going to do?" With my free hand, I fastened and unfastened the bottom button on my sweater.

Ed shook his head. "Remember what you told me—let's not grieve while he's still here."

I tried—and failed—to close my mind's eye.

What Ed had told me about the accident tumbled in my mind. It had been a gorgeous day—unseasonably warm. He, Collin, our twelve-year-old daughter, Katie, and Collin's friend Patrick had been playing basketball in our driveway. The game was rollicking, and Collin laughed and joked with everyone. Afterward, Ed went inside to start dinner and Collin crossed the street to walk his friend to his car. Patrick started the car, and Collin—

I was squeezing Collin's hand. Trying to slow my breathing, I relaxed my grip.

—Collin climbed on the hood of Patrick's car. Patrick drove a few yards, then slammed on his brakes. Holding a Sprite, Collin lost his hold and slid off, hitting the back of his head on the pavement. He lay in the street, dazed, blood flowing from his right ear, his nose, his mouth, his head.

I should have been there. Why had I stayed after school to help the other teachers with their computers when my children needed me? I shook my head. Ed had been there, right there, and it hadn't made any difference.

My head pounded. I needed some Advil. *Oh my God,* I thought. *I'm whining about my little headache. Probably a three in cranial pressure. Oh, Collin, Collin.* I traced his eyebrows with my finger.

A machine screamed. I jumped and my nails tattooed Ed's back.

"Everything's okay," Tammy said. "It's just time for more fluids." She pushed some buttons on the monitor and the noise stopped. Collin seemed unchanged, and I let out my breath. Tammy hung a new IV bag.

"Hey, Collin, Sweetie." I leaned close to his face, wondering whether he could hear me. "Mommy and Daddy are here." I rolled my eyes at myself. Collin had outgrown "Mommy" and "Daddy" ten years ago. I took a deep breath. "We love you, Collin. You get better and come back to us. Rest and let your body fix itself. Then you can wake up and come home."

Too soon, Tammy asked us to leave while she changed Collin's dressings. In the hall, I sagged against the wall and Ed put his arms around me. We rocked back and forth, clutching each other, our bodies convulsing, our grief a banshee careening through the silent corridor, screaming our own fear back at us.

Thursday, March 26

I sat sideways in a blue cloth chair, my head tilted back against the wall, my right leg a jackhammer. Tammy had gone off duty after her twelve-hour shift, and the new nurse—Linda? I couldn't remember her name—had kicked us out of Collin's room nearly an hour before, promising she would come get us "in a few minutes." I fretted about whether she remembered we had moved to a different room.

So many family members and friends had crowded into the tiny Neuro CCU waiting room that the staff had upgraded us to our own, larger space farther down the hall. This room had chairs that opened to cots and a bathroom with a shower. I barely noticed the dozen or so friends and relatives who milled about or sat on the hard vinyl couches. My eyes were fixed on the door. I shot up as it opened, then slumped back down—only more visitors.

Collin's catastrophe had triggered a staggering outpouring of support from our family and friends. A dozen loved ones trickled into the waiting room while our son was in surgery. My cousin Kim agonized with me as I whispered my terror: "How will we survive if Collin dies?" My sister traveled from Fort Lauderdale and my brother from Virginia. Our friends and former next-door neighbors (he was Collin's godfather; their son Jonathan was one of Collin's best friends) also arrived from Virginia. Our parents came and stayed most days, acting as hosts for other well-wishers since Ed and I spent most of our time sequestered in Collin's room. Ed's sisters and their families and our cousins, aunts, and uncles kept a vigil with us.

We tried to send home our former next-door neighbors as soon as they appeared in the waiting room. Their son, Jarett, was born six weeks after our Matt; he'd grown up with our boys and worked beside them as part of Ed's summer painting crew. He had just been released from the hospital himself after receiving a kidney from his father. His parents, Dave and Joanne, had tried to talk him into staying home, worried that an infection might trigger organ rejection, but he insisted on coming.

Other friends enveloped us in hugs and cried with us. Neighbors visited, as did Ed's employees and my colleagues. Collin's supervisor at Best Buy brought an envelope of cash that Collin's co-workers had collected. Cards, flowers, and food filled the room. I was so grateful to these people who had always loved us and whose presence buoyed us in the face of tragedy. But at that moment, the only face I wanted to see was that of the nurse inviting us back into our son's room.

I worried a rosary with tan-colored wooden beads. MaryAnne, a colleague at my school, had given it to me two years earlier after we had talked about ways Tourette Syndrome (TS) bedeviled Collin.

A neurological disorder characterized by motor and vocal tics, TS is often accompanied by co-occurring psychiatric or developmental conditions that sometimes pose bigger challenges than the blinking and sniffing. It had tormented Collin since age three, when our tender toddler morphed into the Incredible Hulk. Neither Ed nor I had ever heard of TS. It hadn't yet become a fixture on TV medical dramas. Clueless about our son's extreme behaviors, we became increasingly exasperated as behavior modification and disciplinary techniques that worked on his brother and sister and my students proved useless on him.

During a ride home to Delaware from Niagara Falls, five-year-old Collin echoed everything anyone said, grunted and sniffed, and said "eggy-eggy-eggy" a thousand times. He bounced in his seat like a windup toy and poked and kicked his older brother and baby sister.

Because Collin's tics were mild, his pediatrician dismissed them as transient and recommended Ritalin. We resisted (and later learned that the drug is contraindicated for TS, as it can cause tardive dyskinesia, a permanent movement disorder), certain more was going on with our son than attention-deficit disorder. We observed evolving tics, obsessive-compulsive behaviors, auditory processing difficulties, and rages that went on and on until Collin wore himself out and fell asleep. With no Google back in the 1980s, research was difficult, but our search convinced us he had TS. An evaluation at the Child Study Center at the Yale University School of Medicine (YCCC) confirmed our diagnosis and determined that—bonus!—our five-year-old was also clinically depressed.

As we were unwilling to move to Connecticut to get appropriate treatment for our son, the doctors referred us to the head of child and adolescent psychiatry at Johns Hopkins, who had previously worked at YCCC. Every two weeks for the next six years, we drove two-and-a-half hours round trip to Baltimore for Collin to see Dr. W. He developed a medication regimen for Collin and taught us to deal with TS's shifting manifestations. A guru even then, Dr. W. is now a world-renowned expert on TS.

Dr. W. had treated Ed and me as partners in Collin's treatment. He had even complimented me on my level-headed, scientific approach. *He wouldn't recognize me now,* I thought, *sitting here wild-eyed, clutching a rosary.*

While on a trip to Mexico, MaryAnne had gotten the rosary blessed for Collin at the Shrine of the Virgin of Guadeloupe. Appreciative but skeptical, I kept forgetting to take it out of my coat pocket. Eventually, though, every time I touched the rosary, usually during recess duty, I said a little prayer for Collin, though I had never learned the actual devotions. What could it hurt? A few months later, except for some twitching and eye blinking, his symptoms disappeared. Last winter, thinking Collin didn't need the rosary anymore, I gave it to Aunt Sal, who had breast cancer. Last night around two a.m. I sent my brother, Jeff, to retrieve it. I rolled each tiny ball between my fingers as I waited to return the magic beads to Collin.

I couldn't wait any longer.

Collin's head was freshly bandaged and he wore a clean gown, but dried blood still painted his face. His lips were dry and cracked. The number in red on the cranial pressure monitor held steady at 101, where it had been all day. I willed it down. A segment on some TV newsmagazine—*Dateline?*—had profiled people who controlled machines with their minds. The number changed to 100. I jumped back, as if the monitor had sent out an electrical shock. Although I concentrated on the number for several minutes, it didn't change. I sighed. Even if my will could affect the machine, would I be making Collin better or just changing the digits?

I tucked the rosary into a pocket on the front of Collin's hospital gown, leaving the crucifix hanging over the top, and then smoothed some Chap-Stik over his lips.

The door to Collin's room swished open, and Patrick's sister, Lee, entered, carrying a vase of flowers.

Nurse Linda flew to intercept her. "No flowers in the Neuro CCU!"

Eyes wide, Lee backed from the room.

Flowers. Collin always brought me flowers when he was a little boy. Early each spring, he'd gather a tiny nosegay of the miniature white flowers that popped up overnight to create a lace coverlet for the backyard. I saw six-year-old Collin in my mind—jeans with holes in the knees sagging below his skinny hips before this was fashionable, grubby fingers, and a dirty-faced smile as he took a respite from playing to bring me a bouquet.

I smiled. Collin was always thoughtful like that. I taught him to drive a stick shift (and like his brother before him, he burned out the clutch on our Prelude in the process). The first night he drove all by himself, he surprised me with my favorite Breyer's mint chocolate chip ice cream. When we purchased a mobile home near the beach, he and Katie contributed its first decorations. Collin was always the last one downstairs on Christmas morning—Matt and Katie always yelled at him—because he wouldn't come down without his presents for all of us.

But Collin's legendary bigheartedness extended beyond material gifts to a generosity of spirit that raised others up. His friend Giancarlo said Collin helped him and others in their chemistry class understand difficult concepts and taught him to play baseball, taking him to the batting cages and showing him how to hit. Giancarlo's mother, Antoinette, told me that when she didn't have a car, Collin was always willing to pick up her daughter and Katie at school and that he always listened patiently when she spoke—unlike her kids, who told her she talked too much!

This was a bigger deal than it sounds, as Collin rarely listened without arguing. His kindness was eclipsed only by his expertise on every subject and his propensity for drawing anyone nearby into an unwinnable argument. The exchanges were often loud, but never boasting or nasty. Collin simply believed he had the more relevant facts. "You just had to admire that," said his cousin Hunter, a favorite debating partner. Eventually, we all learned to extricate ourselves from protracted disputes by cutting him off with, "You're right, Collin!"

"You're right, Collin!" I whispered. "You were always right."

Late that night, the new nurse, Patricia, arranged items to bathe Collin and accepted my offer (plea?) to help. She showed me how to soap and rinse without turning the bed into a swimming pool. Squeezing a washcloth in a basin of warm water, I wiped my son's face.

"I haven't done this in a long time," I said to him as I dabbed the cloth over the soft blond whiskers on his chin. The smell of the soap triggered a picture in my mind of baby Collin splashing and babbling in his bath. I wiped the blood from his nose and ear. "My handsome Collin," I said. "Perfect nose, clear blue eyes. And that smile—you always smile with your whole face. Even your teeth are perfect—you never needed braces." I rinsed the cloth in the basin and tenderly washed his arms and shoulders. Collin's skin felt baby-smooth. It had always amazed me that such a rough-and-tumble boy could have such soft skin. A single small scrape marred his right shoulder. From the fall, I realized, my throat catching.

"Déjà vu all over again," I said, quoting one of Collin's sports idols, New York Yankees Hall of Famer Yogi Berra. "Me cleaning up your cuts and scrapes." I sighed. "Remember the time you got stuck in the sticker bushes in the woods? The boys had to come get me because they couldn't untangle you. We used an entire tube of Neosporin that day." I loosened the gown and washed Collin's chest, maneuvering the cloth around the EKG leads that dotted it. "You've had thousands of cuts and scrapes and bruises and you were always fine. Now you have one little fall, one scratch—" I paused to blink back tears and regain my control. "You'll be fine, Sweetie. I know it. It was just a fall. You'll wake up and ask what all the fuss was. You have to. We need you." *I can't live without you,* I added silently.

Too overcome with emotion to do any more, I kissed my son and let the nurse finish bathing and dressing him. Later, as I rearranged the rosary in the pocket of his fresh gown, I recalled a long-forgotten memory of Collin's other pocket dwellers. He enjoyed catching snakes and salamanders in the backyard, so I always had to check his pockets before doing the laundry.

I regarded the rosary, feeling like a hypocrite, but afraid not to have it. Collin's pressure dropped another point. I pressed my face against his.

"You can fix this, Collin," I whispered, squeezing his hand. "Fix it and come back to us. I know you can do it."

Friday, March 27

As we entered Collin's room, a machine wailed. I waited for someone to reset it, as usual. Then I realized the nurse was not in the room.

The machine continued to scream, but it seemed only Ed and I heard it. I ground my fist against the basketball in my chest. I didn't understand. The nurses never left him alone, even eating their lunch in his room. Collin's blood pressure dropped—ninety . . . eighty . . . seventy. . . . I pointed to the monitor in alarm, unable to speak. Ed ran out into the corridor. Sixty . . . fifty . . . forty—

A woman in scrubs followed Ed into the room. She punched buttons on the monitor and released a clamp on an IV, and the beeping stopped. I studied the monitor. Fifty . . . sixty. . . . I breathed again. I sat down and lay my head on Collin's chest, my tears soaking his gown. *Oh, Collin, won't you wake up? There's so much you haven't done. You need to kiss a girl, hit a home run, graduate next year and go to college. Grandfather already bought a University of Tennessee hat for you. We need to see you on TV, announcing the World Series for ESPN. You need to have babies . . .*

Although I tried not to cry in Collin's presence, my famous control slipped away a bit more each day. I hadn't slept or showered since Wednesday, and the few bites my family had pressed me to eat had left me nauseated. Time sneered, hurtling by at Collin's bedside and standing still when we stalked the clock hands in the waiting room.

I looked Collin over, the way you do a newborn, to check whether he has all his fingers and toes, and saw that his head bandage was askew. It usually covered his left ear, but today, the ear was exposed, along with a row of coarse black sutures just behind it that ran toward the back of his head. I gasped. *Frankenstein. They gave my son Frankenstein stitches.* This was where the neurosurgeon had removed a chunk of Collin's skull to relieve pressure on his swollen brain. I ran my finger along the angry, bumpy line, then tugged gently at the bottom of the dressing to see if it had simply slid up. It didn't budge.

"One more thing they can tease you about, huh, Collin?" I bit my lower lip. In middle school, some students had pantomimed his tics and called him "retard."

This was the boy who, at age ten, held his own in a debate on JFK assassination conspiracy theories with an author who had spent ten years researching the subject. The man gifted Collin an autographed copy of his book. By sixteen, he designed his own video games. But so many days, he had come home from school brimming with hurt and anger. Middle schoolers could be cruel.

Luckily, Collin had fast friends among his cousins and the neighborhood boys he had grown up with. He and Matt spent many days at my cousin Kim's house, playing army with her sons, Paul and Hunter. One time Hunter swore he wouldn't play with Collin anymore because when he shot him, Collin refused to die. He and Collin left their *Sim City* video game running all night, and by morning they'd struck it rich. Both were obsessed with baseball and argued—loudly—over their favorite players' stats. Once Collin had a car, he and Hunter packed the Prelude full of gear and headed for the batting cages.

The 80s were an idyllic time for our sons. Half a dozen other boys Matt's and Collin's ages lived on our street. In the summer, they survived outside sunup to sundown, playing Major League Baseball in our backyard, riding their bikes to the park, enacting a tamer version of *Lord of the Flies* at their fort in the woods, swimming in Giancarlo's pool, playing Ghosts in the Graveyard at dusk. Some of the boys joined us at our beach place, where they hopped the bus to the boardwalk to buy pizza and Italian ice, amass tickets at the arcade, and pretend they weren't scared on the rides.

It wasn't until a year ago that Collin had begun to blossom socially beyond his core group. He learned to drive, got a job at Best Buy, became a writer and broadcaster for his school's radio station, and earned a spot on the honor roll. He had made new friends for the first time in years, several on the McKean High School baseball team. The players planned to visit later, after their game—a game Collin should have played in. I didn't want his friends and teammates to see him with Frankenstein stitches.

The nurse (as they cycled in and out, I lost track of their names) had just finished adjusting the bandage when Dr. B. came in. He nodded at us, his dark eyes hooded and his face a mask, and said there was nothing else he could do for Collin. We had to wait for the brain swelling to go down. He asked permission to do a brain scan to ascertain whether there was any blood flow in Collin's brain.

My body tingled and trembled as the terror returned. I clutched Ed's arms and pulled him aside. "I just can't deal with it today," I pleaded. "It's too soon. I need another day. If it's bad and they want to turn him off—"

The doctor agreed to wait until the next day to do the scan, then left. I lay my head on Collin's chest to hear his heartbeat. Steady and strong, it sounded mechanical. Damned coma. "Collin, please come back to us," I whispered, as I patted his chest.

The rosary was gone.

I rooted in Collin's bedclothes and Ed looked on the floor under the bed. The nurse said she had changed Collin's gown and went to look in the laundry. I began to pace. How could we lose it? This was a bad sign.

What was I doing? Ranting about rosaries and signs—I had never believed in this stuff. And why would I think God might listen to me when I hadn't been to Mass since—when? My brother's wedding twelve years ago? What a phony. A lapsed Catholic, I had only ever done the minimum required by CCD[2] and my father, and after my confirmation I quit going altogether. Periodically I sang in the Methodist church choir my mother directed but was motivated more by pleasing her and loving the music than by the religious rites or sermons.

I had never prayed—really prayed—in my life. Why should God listen to me now? Whenever we ended up in a church, Ed joked that God would smite me. Now I grasped at religion, desperate for it to save my son.

Just then the nurse returned, holding the rosary.

"Thank God," I whispered, and immediately cringed at my own hypocrisy. I returned the beads to Collin's pocket, leaving the crucifix hanging over the front.

I began to massage Collin's feet. Oh, Collin, I am so sorry. Tourette's tortured us all, but especially you. Now this. . . . Dammit, God! He's had enough!

---

[2] Confraternity of Christian Doctrine: the Catholic version of Sunday School.

Was this my punishment for being a lousy mom? For not understanding enough about what he had endured? My cheeks reddened as I recalled the terrible argument Collin and I had had a year before—I couldn't remember now what it had been about. He yelled that he hated me. Frustration trumped control, and I screamed back that I hated him, too.

"One time," I whispered. "It was just one time. All the thousands of times I said 'I love you' will never erase that one angry outburst, will they? I didn't mean it. Things were so intense all the time . . ." I stroked his arm. *Through it all*, I said silently, *I've always been so proud of you—how you dealt with your Tourette's, the time you volunteered to set up the computer lab at my school, how you taught Katie her times tables—*

I looked up as people streamed into the room. Aunt Sal had organized a coast-to-coast prayer vigil for Collin. Ed's and my families and friends had been wonderful, sitting hour after hour on stiff sofas in the featureless waiting room, taking their turns to see Collin, comforting Matt and Katie. They had prepared meals, returned Ed's business phone calls, even fed our dogs and cats, who must have thought we abandoned them. Now, about twenty of us crowded into Collin's hospital room and held hands in a circle around him, enveloping him in our hope.

Someone began to pray. I said the Our Father but couldn't remember all the words to the Hail Mary, a prayer I had said hundreds of times in confession as a kid. *Bless me Father, for I have sinned.* . . . What other prayers did I know? *I believe in God, the Father almighty.* . . . What was the rest? I begged shamelessly for a good outcome from the brain scan that loomed like a specter. I wondered if my clumsy prayers helped Collin or just pissed God off.

Saturday, March 28

We sat in the waiting room, again—breath bated, pending the results of Collin's brain scan. For the first half-hour I had paced. Now I curled like a fetus in a chair, eyes closed, arm covering my face. Thudding in my chest blocked the murmured conversations around me, and each beat felt like an assault. I could feel the outline of my heart, hard and stretched tight, ready to burst, a basketball filled with too much air—the slightest bounce, and it would explode. This must be how we got the term, broken heart. *Please, please, please, God. Let him be okay. Let him come back to us. Let us have our miracle. I'll go back to church. Work at a homeless shelter. I won't yell at my kids. Anything.*

These past three days, as I sat silently by Collin's side for hours on end, thoughts had conducted a military-grade bombardment, alternately terrorizing me with death scenarios and calming me with vivid memories. Now I shook my head in disbelief as a biblical stream of consciousness wound its way through my mind. I had thought about God and religion more this week than in decades.

"The Story of Abraham" flashed as if on a marquee. At God's command, Abraham took his son, Isaac, to the top of a mountain and prepared to sacrifice him. As Abraham raised his knife, God said never mind—it was just a test of faith. *Like those Emergency Broadcasting tones on the radio,* I thought. "This has been a test. . . ." Was this my test of faith?

I took a deep breath. Better to be covered, just in case. Leaving the floor for the first time, I took the elevator down. Piano music floated through the main corridor—Tchaikovsky's "Pathétique," the music I grew up with. I listened a moment, then entered the chapel. The door sucked closed behind me, and the room became a soundproof booth. No more bustle of people scurrying down the hallway, no more music, no beeps and screams of machines. Just God and me.

Neither of us spoke.

Small, plain, dark, the chapel neither welcomed nor comforted. My gaze was drawn to a book that lay open on a lectern at the front of the room. A prayer log—you begged for your miracle, and others who read your message could pray for your loved one.

I felt combative, defiant. *How many people had their prayers answered?* I gritted my teeth, then scrawled beneath the last entry, "Okay, God, go ahead. If you really, truly need him, want him more than I do, take him. I put my son into your hands."

A surge of smug relief flooded over me as I exhaled three days' anxiety. Collin would be fine. No one, not even God, could need him, want him, more than his mother. I stomped back to the elevator without noticing whether music played or not.

As I opened the waiting room door, a magazine blared at me from a holder bolted to the wall across the room. The only periodical in the rack, its cover headline, in six-inch letters, leapt out at me—*Faith*.[3]

I braced myself in the doorway, gaping. Faith? I come back from sparring with God and that's the first thing I see? Too weird to be a coincidence—must be a sign. If I am strong and have faith, Collin will be all right!

Or was it mocking me? Jesus—signs, coincidences. . . . I was losing it. I'm going crazy. Collin will come home and they'll send me to the nuthouse.

I jumped as Nurse Pat touched my shoulder. "We're ready for you."

Ed and I followed her to a tiny cubicle across the hall from Collin's room. Dr. B. and the neurologist sat at a table. The neurosurgeon nodded at us and opened a folder.

He's not looking at us again.

"As I explained before, this test shows us the blood flow in different areas of the brain," he began.

Come on, come on! Is my son still alive? My heels drummed on the floor.

"Where there is no blood flow, the cells die," he continued.

Yes, and—? I pressed my hand to my chest. *Don't let the ball bounce,* I told myself. *Stop torturing us! Come on, God, we have a deal—*

"We found zero blood flow here and here, and ten percent flow in these areas." He indicated several sections on the scan. "That's it. It doesn't look promising. I'm sorry."

---

[3] I could not find this magazine cover to validate my narrative. I did find *Time's* "Faith and Healing," June 1996, but I don't think that was the one. I know I didn't imagine it, as it cropped up several times.

Yes! He's still alive! We got our miracle. Thank you, God. I just had to have faith. Collin will be okay. He's still here! Tears flowed down my face—tears of joy, I convinced myself.

Dr. B. told us they would start to bring Collin out of his coma. It would take four or five days, and Collin probably would stay stable during that process.

I couldn't wait to tell the others who awaited the news. I couldn't wait to get back to Collin.

Bursting from the airless cell, I crashed into the arms of Reverend Baker. A longtime family friend, the elderly Methodist pastor had co-officiated at Ed's and my wedding. One of those rare preachers, his sermons resonated with me. The minister enveloped me in a bear hug so tight I could barely breathe. He asked about the brain scan, and I related what the doctors had told us.

"That's great news," he said into my ear. "Collin is such a wonderful boy. You know Flo and I have been praying for him and for your family."

I nodded against his shoulder, tears flowing. "Is this our miracle?"

"Our faith is strong," he said.

"This has been such a test of faith," I said, "but I'm afraid this isn't the real test."

Rev. Baker held me away from him and looked at me with sad eyes. He nodded, then crushed me in his embrace again.

I peeled myself away and hurried to the waiting room. "He's still alive!" I burst out. "Brain activity is minimal, but they can't turn him off! Collin has more time!"

Everyone hugged and the room filled with excited chatter. I slipped out, headed to the Neuro CCU. My school principal, Judy, intercepted me and insisted she had to talk to me immediately. Desperate to see Collin, I brought her into his room with me.

Judy told me she had had a vision of Collin. She wasn't smiling.

My face fell. "You didn't see him getting better."

"I thought he was already gone."

No! No! Allow me this moment!

"On my way here, I had the radio on," Judy said. "The song from Titanic came on—you know, 'My Heart Will Go On'—

I fixed my eyes on Collin as "my heart will go on and on" looped through my brain.

"—and I knew it was a sign Collin can help other people if you donate his organs—"

"He's not dead yet," I said through my teeth.

The previous day, without anyone asking, we had told Nurse Pat he was an organ donor. I don't know why I was so eager to share that—I think I was just proud of him. When I took him to get his driver's license, Collin checked the organ donor box all on his own. We discussed what that entailed, and he reaffirmed his choice.

Ed and I had told Pat we would honor Collin's decision, if it came to that. Now the reality of his decision—and ours—sent waves of terror buzzing through my body.

Judy moved to the corner to say a rosary for Collin. I sat by my son.

"Oh, Collin," I whispered, stroking and kissing his face, "Now you can work on getting better. We've got our miracle."

As I smoothed Collin's sheet, I planted tiny kisses on his cheeks. "You 'bout gave me a heart attack. You always did know how to take us on a wild ride. Remember when I taught you to drive and you almost missed the curve on Stoney Batter? I grabbed the wheel and you got so mad! And you somehow managed to bend an axle on the Prelude when you hit a curb. I thought if you ever ended up in the hospital it would be because of your driving, not something like this."

As I massaged my son's hand, I once again willed the cranial pressure to drop. Ninety-four—going down. "Fight hard, Collin," I said. "Come back to us. If you get better and wake up, you can have anything you want. Name it. A new Super Sega Nintendo Twenty-seven, a new Mac with a thousand Gigs of memory—anything! I'll clean your room for you every day. You'll never have to do dishes again. We'll find a way to get you the Hummer you love. You're the only thing that's important. We need you."

Pat readied a new syringe to inject into Collin's IV. She smiled with her mouth and nodded toward the door.

Swearing silently, I made myself stand. "She's kicking me out again," I whispered to Collin. "I'll take a shower and then I'll be back. You work on getting better."

Sunday, March 29

I woke with a start. The nurse had evicted me around four a.m. and I had fallen asleep on a chair that opened to a bed. *Collin!* Then I relaxed. *They would have come to wake us. . . .* What time was it? The sun was just burning off an early morning fog. I lay back down, still exhausted.

Ed slept next to me, his slim frame sprawled over a chair. Although the temperature soared into the 80s with beautiful, clear skies, Matt and Katie had refused to leave the hospital during the day, going home only to sleep. This week had been so hard on them. Matt had been sullen and irritable and resisted the comfort of family and friends, sitting alone or taking walks when not at Collin's side. Katie had avoided Collin's room, surrounding herself with friends. She had witnessed the accident and held Collin's head in her lap, blood soaking her clothes, until the ambulance arrived. I squeezed my eyes closed. Such a burden for a twelve-year-old.

While I focused so desperately on Collin, I had neglected my other children. At one point I sat them down and apologized.

"We're fine," they insisted.

"If either of you were lying in that hospital bed, you know I would be doing the same for you, right?"

Matt and Katie nodded, eyes down, and returned to their friends.

Their buddies kept a vigil with them in the small waiting room in which we had first been closeted, and they passed the time playing cards. Nurse Pat tried to get them to open up to her about their feelings and offered to answer their questions, but they demurred. Collin's high school principal shook his head when he encountered the group.

"So that's it," he said. "At school we announced that students upset over Collin's accident could come to the auditorium, but no one showed. Now I understand—they're all here."

For a moment everything seemed so peaceful. But what a fragile peace. I had a sudden desperate desire to hold my children—to stroke their hair, to breathe their fresh innocence, to shield them from this horror.

34

Where are you, God? What kind of God allows a boy to suffer this way? Didn't you hear our prayers? What—it's Sunday, day of rest? Too busy to bother with one faithless family? I cringed as my mind replayed the TV commercial in which the guardian angel gets distracted and a piano falls on his charge. Where was Collin's guardian angel?

With Ed still asleep, I went to the bathroom and brushed my teeth. As I sank back into a chair, I saw it again—*Faith*. That damned magazine haunted me. I stomped across the room, tore it from the rack, and flipped it so the cover faced the wall. Then I sat in a different chair. I didn't need that today. Why did faith come so easily to some people while I was cynical and skeptical? If God existed, he (she?) must have seen through my act when I tried to believe that I believed. But then he or she also knew I've tried everything I know—doctors, prayer, force of will—to save my son.

I shifted in my chair, and an uncomfortable prickliness nagged at me. Not the ache in my bones, not even the cranial pressure—the number had fallen to eighty-nine. No, I had the sense that something about Collin had changed. Nothing specific, just a Spidey-sense, the way I could always tell when the kids were coming down with a fever even before they felt hot. Like the premonition of impending doom that had struck me—and my mother—when Collin was born. My other children's births hadn't evoked anything similar. Over the years I had dismissed it as mother's worry, but what if—? What if this was his destiny? What if he had done all he was supposed to do? He struggled so hard and accomplished so much—

I had proofread an essay for Collin a few months before about his favorite sports figure, Cal Ripken. One line settled into my heart. Collin had written that Ripken's perseverance had inspired him to do what he loved and not quit despite "insurmountable odds." What if Collin's job had been to conquer those seemingly insurmountable odds, and now that he had completed his mission, he got to leave this painful world? What if death wasn't a punishment, but a Golden Ticket—?[4]

---

[4] A pass that admits its holder into the magical factory in Roald Dahl's *Willie Wonka and the Chocolate Factory.*

Right, I thought, shaking my head. I sounded like a televangelist—or maybe a cult leader. What was wrong with me? How could I think such things? Faith. I had to keep the faith. Damned magazine. The pressure kept dropping. Collin was getting better. They were bringing him out of the coma and he would wake up soon and laugh away our worry.

Sure, my mind mocked.

Rising, I walked to the window. In the still-dim room light, I shielded my eyes against the brilliance. The fog had cleared (at least from the sky), and the day promised a reprise of the glorious weather on the day of the accident. I spun away from the view.

Ed sat up and rubbed the sleep from his eyes. Wordlessly, we followed the well-worn trail to our son.

It disturbed me to see Collin so still. Four days, and not even an eye twitch. Our Collin was never still. Even when he slept he wiggled and jerked. Now I'd cut off my arm to see a tic. I'd take his place if he'd just open his eyes, move a finger or a toe. . . . And he never slept through the night, much less for four days straight. He'd sit on the floor in his bedroom at three a.m., reading about garter snakes in the *World Book.* I used to yell at him for being up. Had he known all along he had no time to waste sleeping?

I looked up to see Collin's best friends—Peter, Jonathan, and Giancarlo—in the doorway.

The boys had grown up with Collin and had spent so much time at our home that I jokingly called them my other sons. Paul, George, and Ringo, with Collin as John, the leader. They had parked themselves in the waiting room since Wednesday, going home to sleep only at our insistence. Although each had visited Collin, this was the first time the band had gotten back together.

As Ed and I hugged each boy, a video looped in my mind—the four playing baseball in our backyard, permanent bases worn into the lawn (this always amused my friend Gail, who had girls). . . . The beeps and incessant music from Nintendo and the countless paper scraps with game tips—cheats—I had picked up from the floor. . . . Ed ranting as shovels and hammers disappeared one by one to the boys' fort in the woods. The boys fought sometimes but observed the code of *omertà*[5] when I tried to intervene. One would stomp off, returning an hour later to discover what new adventure Collin had conjured up. These boys had never abandoned Collin when others tormented him. They adored him.

I swallowed hard and looked each boy in the eye. "Whatever you want to say to him, make sure you say it. The doctors tell us he's probably going to die." My mouth gaped open. I couldn't believe I said it out loud.

The boys stood rock-still. All three began to cry unashamedly. They formed a semicircle at the foot of Collin's bed.

Ed and I slipped out into the hallway. We stood apart, weeping the tears of Niobe[6] for all our boys.

Later that night, Ed and I were by Collin's side when the neurosurgical resident came in. Small and bony with short dark hair, she nodded to us without making eye contact, her face expressionless, and began to examine Collin.

She never speaks to us, I thought, annoyed. Skullface. Must have practiced her bedside manner at Dr. Mengele's knee. "How is he doing?" I asked. "His cranial pressure is down to ninety-two . . ."

"That doesn't mean a thing," the resident said, her eyes on Collin's chart.

Wait . . . what?! I sat back in my chair, stunned. I've concentrated on this machine for four days and it doesn't mean a thing?!

The resident pushed a button to lower the head of Collin's bed. As it went down, the pressure number went up—ninety-four . . . ninety-five . . . ninety-seven—

"Stop it!" I said. "Put him back up!"

"I'm telling you it doesn't matter," the resident said. "The swelling has severely diminished blood flow to most of his brain. The lights are on, but we don't know if anyone's home."

---

[5] Mafia code of silence.

[6] In Greek mythology, Niobe boasted about her six sons and six daughters. As punishment for her pride, Leto, the goddess of motherhood, sent her two children, Apollo and Artemis, to kill them. Niobe prayed for relief from her suffering, and Zeus turned her into a rock that weeps when the snow melts above it.

I stood up, trembling. I wanted to scream at her, to throw her to the floor and stomp on her face. Instead, I stared openmouthed as she skulked from the room without another word. Collapsing into my chair, I shook with impotent rage.

It Ends

Monday, March 30, 1998

*B*ring me my gray sweats and clean underwear," I said to Ed. We stood in the waiting room, of course. Ed was preparing to leave the hospital. The doctors expected Collin to remain stable for a few days, and the aimless hanging around had been stressful for Matt and Katie. We had decided they should go back to school. Katie had balked, and Ed said he would take her.

I walked him to the door and kissed him goodbye. It was the first time in five days I had been alone, and I felt as empty as the room. The magazine rack still mocked me. Someone had turned the magazine back around. I only wished.

"Faith," I said aloud. Hmmph. Had I been naïve all along, pretending to believe in miracles like Professor Marvel in *The Wizard of Oz?* I had been so sure we had gotten another sign . . .

The day before, my mother had burst into the room, excited after having met a family in the elevator. Her words tumbled out in a rush.

"The son was about Collin's age. He had orange hair, tattoos up and down his arms, and everything that could be pierced was. His mother and I started talking. The boy fell off his skateboard and hit the back of his head, just like Collin, and was in a coma—and he's fine now!" She clasped her hands and smiled, but her upturned mouth didn't match her too-bright eyes and furrowed brow.

Why would Mom have met them, if not to give us hope? Was this another cruel joke? I scowled at the magazine. Was I stupid to hope for a miracle? Maybe the only miracle was Collin's life.

"Why am I being so negative?" I said out loud. "He's getting better." Collin's cranial pressure had dropped all day Sunday. It flirted with eighty when the nurse banished me. I strode to Collin's room—

—and stopped short in the doorway.

Collin looked as placid as ever, and the monitors beat their same synthesized "Tubular Bells" rhythm. But panic welled from my gut and gripped my limbs. *This is it.* I drew a long, halting breath.

Walking to my son's side, I caressed his face. "Hi, Sweetie, I'm here." Suddenly my muscles turned to Jell-O and my whole body ached. I clutched his hand and, out of habit, checked the cranial pressure. Eighty-four . . . eighty-five.

My hand on Collin's chest didn't seem to belong to me, but floated in slow motion, like an overexposed film in which each frame blurs into the next. Collin's heart felt strong, his breathing regular. Still, I had an overwhelming sense of . . . what? Grief. Pain. Was Collin in pain? They said he couldn't feel any pain . . .

The monitor read eighty-seven. Blood pressure one-forty over forty.

I ran to the waiting room and dialed Ed's cell phone. "Come back," I said. "Right now. It's okay, Collin's okay—nothing's happened, but you need to be back here. Now. Bring the kids and come back."

Nothing's happened, the echo taunted in my mind. But something *had* happened—just nothing anyone could see, nothing the machines could measure, other than a slight increase in cranial pressure—which Dr. Mengele had said meant nothing. Why hadn't I checked on Collin before Ed left? I would never have let him leave. *No one has noticed anything wrong,* I thought. There was nothing to notice. I just *knew.*

I went back to Collin's room and stood looking at him as tears streamed down my cheeks.

Nurse Pat touched my arm. "Is there anything I can do for you?"

She knows, too. She's done this before.

I ached to hold Collin in my arms, to cradle and comfort him and promise everything would be all right. That's what moms are supposed to do.

Pat unhooked the EKG leads and slid Collin to one side of the mattress. I climbed onto the bed and lay next to him, wrapping my arm around his chest, laying my head on his shoulder, breathing his scent. As I felt my son's body against mine, alternating waves of memory and agony trembled through me.

I stroked his hair, his cheeks, his chest, as I had when he was an infant. You were such a sweet baby. The easiest birth of all my kids. You never caused me any pain.

"I love you, Collin," I said, my voice breaking. "I'm so sorry you've had to endure this. So much pain for such a tender boy. I've let you down. I didn't protect you. I'm sorry for all the times I lost my temper, the times I didn't understand."

Everything became clear—all the gifts Collin's life had brought me, brought all of us. I was so stupid. But you knew all along, somehow, didn't you? I thought I was teaching you, but you taught me to be patient with a struggling boy, to be tolerant of the teen who marched to a different drummer, sometimes playing in a totally different band. You showed me how to drink in all of life—good and bad. You inspired me to never give up, to never admit defeat. You modeled what's important—not grades or a clean house or being popular, but love.

I kissed my son's cheek. "All I ever needed to do was love you."

Ed and the children had come in. Matt and Katie draped themselves over me, crying. Ed wrapped his arms around us.

I reflected on the deal I had made with God—my test of faith. That wasn't the test at all, was it? It hasn't even begun. The real test begins when the reprieve doesn't come.

I lifted myself up on one elbow so I could look into my son's face. "I want you to come back to us," I whispered. "You've fought hard these past few days, trying to stay here for us. I want you to keep fighting and wake up. But I can feel your torment.

"Collin, my son, treasure of my heart, if this is too hard for you, if you need to go, then go. I release you."

A wisp, like smoke floating up from a candle, appeared between my face and Collin's. It swirled once, brushed my cheek, then sped off into the room and disappeared.

Collin was gone.

Nurse Pat booted us from Collin's room again to perform another brain scan, which confirmed what I already knew. As we sat, dazed, she asked us to meet with a representative from the Gift of Life Donor Program, who would explain the organ donation process. We were escorted into the same closet where we had met with the doctors. It seemed smaller than before—the walls closing in like a real-life *Fermat's Room.*[7] As we all squeezed in around the Formica-topped table, our chair legs shrieked against the floor like fingernails dragged across a chalkboard.

"The doctors will evaluate his organs to make sure they are viable for transplant," the woman said. "Then they will harvest them and they will be delivered for implantation into the recipients. Your son will help many people and save lives."

I flinched at the word "harvest." It sounded so impersonal, so inhuman, something done in the mud on a farm with a great big green tractor. "The corn's ready for harvest." Or, "We had a great soybean harvest this year." Saving other people's lives had seemed such a noble pursuit when it involved simply a box to check on a form. Now, though, the realization glossed over in the DMV office is that to save those lives, our son had to die.

And she hadn't even said Collin's name.

Again there seemed to be no ventilation in the room, and the air settled like a shroud. I struggled to slow my breaths as the rep asked which of our son's organs we were willing to donate. The first few questions pierced my heart—Would we donate Collin's kidneys, lungs, heart?—but I expected them. Pancreas, liver, intestines? Ed gripped my hand. Would we donate Collin's corneas? They would remove both eyes.

Every muscle in my body clenched and burned. Ed and I stared at each other, passing anguish, like the soda can Collin once microwaved, back and forth between us. Our son's beautiful blue eyes—Morse keys that telegraphed his every emotion—could we let

---

[7] A 2007 horror movie in which four strangers must solve puzzles and figure out who is trying to murder them as the walls mechanically close in.

them be cut out? I fought back tears as Ed and I searched each other's faces for a way out, only to capitulate our silent assent.

That's it, I thought—but the woman continued her assault. Would we donate heart valves, blood vessels, connective tissue? Collin's bones? Blindsided by the last image, I crumpled, as if all the air had been sucked from the room. *Maybe we'll just suffocate in here and it will all be over.*

"His bones?!" I croaked. He'd be a rag doll.

"They will harvest [ugh!] the long bones in his legs," she explained.

I folded my arms to stop them from shaking while my heels hammered Bach's "Toccata and Fugue" on the floor.

Would we donate Collin's skin? The woman asked, one body part at a time, whether they could take Collin's skin. From his arms? His legs? His chest? His abdomen? His back? Tears seared my face.

They want to carve up my son like a Thanksgiving turkey. I threw up my hands to make the woman stop, to erase her, and Ed and I clung to each other for a long moment. The rep pointed to where each of us needed to sign the consent form. I scribbled, unseeing, and fled the room.

We had just agreed to let the boy we had poured our souls into for nearly seventeen years—our son in the next room who was still warm and breathing and whose heart pulsed with a strong beat—be butchered.

Ed started the car and backed from the parking space. I looked up at the building in front of us.

Maternity Entrance, I read silently. *We came out the Maternity Entrance.* Suddenly I regretted letting Matt and Katie ride with their grandparents. I needed to hold my babies. I looked down at my hands and turned them over, then back. Then I wrapped my arms around my waist and began to rock ever so slightly.

We rode home in silence, each lost in private despair—unable to help, unable to be helped. I noticed nothing, thought about nothing, all the way up Limestone Road.

As Ed turned into our neighborhood, I was jolted from my catatonia. The cherry trees lining the street had bloomed, and they blazed in a riot of color against the setting sun. It had been winter when I had last been home. Our son died just as the rest of the world was being reborn.

We passed two men lifting a refrigerator into a truck, a woman gardening, and a teenager washing his car. *How can they act so normal? Don't they know everything has changed?*

Ed pulled into the driveway and turned off the ignition. We sat without speaking for a few moments, and then, as if acknowledging some agreement, got out at the same time and stumbled like the walking dead into the silent house.

II
Collin

I saw you dashing into KFC today,
Cargo shorts and flip-flops snow blind;
Ornery hair wagging like tongues taunting
the wind.
Did you see me?

Beautiful Boy

*I*n *Fahrenheit 451,* Ray Bradbury wrote, "Everyone must leave something behind when he dies. . . . A child or a book or a painting or a house or a wall built or a pair of shoes made. Something your hand touched some way so your soul has somewhere to go when you die, and when people look at that tree or that flower you planted, you're there." Collin left many such touchstones.

Collin was a delightful baby, easygoing and loving. He toddled around the yard pushing his green lawn mower, golden curls bouncing, a delighted grin on his face. But about age three, our darling morphed into a dragon. Everything revolved around Collin's moods, as we all learned to avoid the fire that flared when he was provoked—or sometimes for no obvious reason. Any reprimand, frustration, or challenge might prompt vehement arguments or screaming rages that lasted until he wore himself out and fell asleep.

At first we just thought he was being a brat, so we ramped up the discipline. Matt and my students had responded well to my behavior management strategies, but Collin deflected them like a pint-sized Captain America repelling them with his shield. So I read books about parenting. I frustrated a workshop presenter at Matt's school when I insisted that nothing she or the books recommended had any effect on Collin.

When we noticed eye blinks and muscle jerks, our pediatrician dismissed them as "transient tics of childhood." In the mid-eighties, the internet was still a conglomeration of private networks, and the duo who would eventually develop Google was still learning long division. So I talked to people, asked questions, and did library research. Collin's godfather mentioned hearing a radio report about Tourette Syndrome. Although the first case had been reported in 1825, no one I knew had ever heard of it (a spate of TV medical shows featuring individuals cursing uncontrollably, a rare expression of TS called coprolalia, would come much later). The more I read, the more convinced I became that TS was our dragon. When Collin was five, experts at the Yale Child Study Center confirmed my suspicions— and told us he was severely depressed, too.

Tourette Syndrome is a neurological disorder that compels repetitive motor or vocal tics. Although most people's tics are mild, co-occurring behavioral or social challenges can wreak havoc on self-esteem and relationships. Collin had ADHD, a few OCD tendencies, and rages. Dealing with his symptoms and feeling different from other kids triggered depression, which manifested in Collin not as sadness, but as irritability, anger, and sleeplessness.

Every other week for nearly a decade, we drove 130 miles roundtrip to Johns Hopkins Hospital in Baltimore, Maryland, to meet with the head of child and adolescent psychiatry. A TS expert (and today, one of the top two TS experts in the world), Dr. W. talked with Collin, managed antidepressants, and taught us coping strategies such as timeouts instead of spankings. He learned along with us as Prozac masked Collin's inhibitions (remember Roseanne Barr's annihilation of the National Anthem?) and accidental tricyclic overdoses (our fault, not the doctor's) endangered his liver but magically improved his behavior and mood.

The meds were hard to regulate. We would find the perfect dose, and then Collin would grow and throw everything out of whack again. Life was a roller coaster operated by the little girl from a Henry Wadsworth Longfellow poem I used to read to the kids: "When she was good, she was very good indeed, but when she was bad she was horrid."

Collin couldn't play with Matt without an argument. He bossed Katie around and once grabbed her around the neck and choked her. If everyone wanted McDonald's, Collin argued for KFC. Ed and I (mostly me) yelled a lot, punished Collin a lot, struggled to get him through homework without a meltdown, and threatened to throw away the G.I. Joe components that swarmed his floor like army ants—even the battleship that had taken Ed and me hours to assemble late one Christmas eve, thanks to the hundreds of tiny pieces and the thousand decals we had to affix on every surface. Once, in an exasperated rage, I even threw his Nintendo console across his bedroom.

Sometimes I got in the car and just drove, finally pulling into some random parking lot when I could no longer see through my tears. The days leading up to one particular Thanksgiving were so distressing that I called my brother to say we weren't coming after all. My parents, who often rescued us (I was never sure whether it was us from Collin or Collin from us), took the children to Virginia while Ed and I stayed home.

Things were frequently tense, as Collin did nothing halfway. At age eight, he was hospitalized after he said he hated having TS and was going to jump in front of a truck. But the positive aspects of his personality were just as intense. Collin was super smart and lived to learn. An educational diagnostician told us that then-five-year-old Collin would never learn to read, but eight-year-old Collin pored over *National Geographic* and *World Book* when he got sent to his room. No matter the topic, Collin was the expert. Fascinated by animals, he abducted salamanders and snakes, dug up sand crabs, caught sand sharks, and brought home a mangy, flea-infested black kitten he named Sparckey. He also liked to figure out how things worked and could put together thousand-piece G.I. Joe vehicles without the instructions. What were we thinking, putting together that battleship ourselves?

Collin threw himself fully into everything he did, and fun, interesting ideas floated around him like a fog. His enthusiasm was infectious, attracting a posse of neighborhood boys and cousins enthralled by playing army for hours on end, racing each other in *Mario Cart*,[8] and incinerating spiders in our basement (it's a wonder our house is still standing).

When he was "very good indeed," Collin had a great sense of humor, and when he laughed, you could see his tonsils. He was kind, generous, and thoughtful. Embracing our shared love of reading, he frequently suggested books he had read that he thought I might like. After he got his driver's license and a job at Best Buy, he brought me gifts just because. In high school, Collin tutored a friend in math and volunteered as a science aide. Just a few months before he died, he volunteered to singlehandedly set up the new computers for every classroom in my school. The thought he put into every Christmas present was legendary.

When Collin was about fourteen, his tics diminished. TS symptoms often abate at puberty, but more significantly, the co-occurring conditions took ever-longer vacations. Collin was happier and the rages disappeared. As his focus sharpened, his grades improved, and he was named sports director for his school's radio station. Relationships became less fraught, and new friendships, the first since childhood, blossomed. He and Matt started to hang out together. Girls began to notice him—and he them.

Collin's future shone and sparkled like a limitless sun.

Then the storm hit.

My description doesn't begin to reveal the multifaceted individual Collin was. To truly appreciate his huge presence—and to grasp how devastating his loss has been—you need to meet him, see him, hear him. You need to understand what he left behind.

---

[8] A Nintendo car racing video game.

Photographic Memory

Collin is four, standing in the kitchen, the door ajar behind him. His favorite *Trans-formers* T-shirt has faded from washing. Jeans with a hole in the left knee sag beneath skinny hips, showing a strip of pale belly and the top band of *He-Man*[9] tighty-whities a decade before this look is popular. His week-old, too big ("I *need* this size, Mom. My feet are really big!") Nikes are gray, scuffed, and muddy; one is untied. Collin's blond hair is damp over his forehead and ears. A fresh  scratch on his right cheek matches a perpetual purplish-red Juicy Juice mustache. He has been outside catching salamanders—and memories. Collin's clear blue eyes, liquid and luminous, are lit all the way to his heart. His whole-faced smile betrays his secret.

---

[9] A popular animated TV show of the 1980s.

Collin brings his right hand from behind his back and holds it out toward me. "For you," he says. The whole backyard is lodged under his nails, and a white band on his index finger revels in its release from a bothersome Band-Aid. Old scratches create mazes on his arm. In his fist he clutches a spray of tiny flowers, lily-white with five pink-striped petals and long, slender leaves—the Virginia Spring Beauty blossoms that carpet the lawn at the edge of the woods in the spring.

I take them and hug my thanks. Collin breaks away.

"I love you, Mommy!" He spins on one heel and bounds back outside. The door hits the wall and bounces back.

I arrange the nosegay in the smallest glass I can find. Later, at our local arts festival, I buy a tiny ceramic vase. It holds multitudes of buttercups, dandelions, blue cornflowers, and white and purple clover and thistle flowers—and those are just the blooms I can identify. I break out a larger vessel for the tulips and daffodils, forsythia, peonies, mums, hydrangea, and azalea Collin decides look better indoors than out.

"Mom! He's doing it again. Make him stop!" Matthew, seven, squeezes over against the back door of our Accord sedan, folds his arms over his chest, and glares out the window. Five-year-old Collin slides over and erases the new inches between them, then pokes his brother several times in the thigh.

Matthew slaps Collin's hand away. "Mom!"

"Collin, move back over and don't touch your brother," I warn.

Collin moves back to the center of the seat. "I didn't do anything." He taps Matthew's foot with his.

"Cut it out, Collin!" Matthew yells.

"Collin!" I echo, twisting in my seat to up the ante with a hard stare.

Collin grins. His eyes flip up and to the right twice.

I twist back around and exchange a glance with my husband, Ed. It's Labor Day, and we are halfway back to Delaware from Niagara Falls.

"'top, Cowwin!" One-year-old Katie joins the fray. I turn and see Collin waving his hand in front of her face. Again I stare. He grins, his eyes flip, and then he folds his hands in his lap. I turn back.

Katie begins to whine.

"Mom, now he's tickling her!"

"Collin, that's it! Do not touch Matt or Katie!" Ed and I sigh in concert.

"I'm just playing."

"She doesn't want to play."

"Yes, she does." Collin leans over against his sister's car seat, his face an inch from hers. "Don't you, Katie?"

Katie cries.

"Stop arguing," I say.

"I'm not."

"Collin!" I look to Ed for support. He stares at the road.

Katie continues to cry. I unhook my seat belt to find her Hugga Bunch doll among the toys on the floor. She clutches it. Two fingers slide into her mouth and she twirls the doll's curly purple hair with the fingers of her other hand.

"Eggy-eggy-eggy," Collin says. Katie begins to cry again. "Eggy-eggy-eggy."

Matt starts to complain but I beat him to it. "Collin, be quiet! You're driving us crazy!"

"Sniggy-sniggy."

"That's enough!" My voice is getting sharper. I take a breath. "Hey, let's play the license plate game. Who can find the first number one on a license plate?" Katie quiets down.

"There's one!" shouts Matthew.

Collin puts his hand over his brother's eyes.

"Leave me alone!"

"Collin!" Ed finally speaks up. "What's the matter with you? Knock it off!"

Collin begins to move his knees apart and then together, hitting Matt on one side and Katie on the other. "Pop, pop, pop," he says. Both kids yell, and Katie starts to cry again.

I reach back and grab Collin's leg, holding it still.

"Ow! You hurt me! Owwww!"

"I did not. Stop yelling!"

Collin continues to moan and howl, holding his leg and rocking back and forth. Katie is crying and Matt is hunched over with his hands covering his ears.

Five more hours to go. How much prison time would I get for throwing Collin out on the Pennsylvania Turnpike? I look at Ed. He thinks the same thing.

Ed pulls the car over. Matt climbs up front and I squeeze into the back between Katie and Collin. I pick up *Where the Sidewalk Ends* by Shel Silverstein and start reading "Boa Constrictor." Collin snuggles against me and Katie sucks her fingers and twists my hair.

"Matt, try it again." I hold up the flash card.

"I don't know." He looks at his feet.

"Three times four," I repeat.

"Eleven?"

"Three fours," I hint.

No answer.

A few feet away, six-year-old Collin is building a tower out of Construx.

"Geez, Matt," he says. "It's just four plus four plus four—four, eight, twelve." He shakes his head and adds a girder to his construction.

Collin's grandfather shared this memory.

"Not all spiders make webs," says Collin. "The trap door spider hides in a hole in the ground and when some prey comes by, he jumps out." He acts out the spider's pounce.

"How do you know so much about spiders and snakes and other animals?" Grandfather asks.

"Well, when I get sent to my room, I read the encyclopedias on my bookshelf." He blushes. "I get sent to my room a lot."

"We know you are interested in animals and history," says Grammy, giving him a hug. "Would you like a subscription to *National Geographic Kids?*"

"Yes. But I want the one Grandfather gets—the yellow one."

"You're only eight," says Grandfather. "Are you sure you can read the regular one? It might be too hard for you."

"It's not too hard." Collin goes to his grandparents' magazine rack and picks out a *National Geographic,* opens to a page, and begins to read, fluently.

Grandfather whistles and puts his arm around Collin's waist. "The yellow one it will be."

"I'm safe!" Collin yells. He stomps the patch of dirt in the center of our backyard that serves as a permanent second base.

"Out!" yells Matthew. He tosses the baseball into the air.

"Yeah, Collin," says Jonathan. "You were out."

"Was not! The ball wasn't here yet when I touched the base!"

"I got you on your back! You're out!" yells Matthew. He tags Collin again.

"You're an asshole!" Collin yells back, fists clenched. "You just think because you're twelve you're in charge."

"Collin, just play," says Peter from behind the plate. "It doesn't matter."

"No! I'm not out! You guys always call me out on purpose!"

"We call you out because you're out," says Matthew. "Dad, Collin's being a jerk."

On the deck, Ed puts down his newspaper with a sigh. "Collin, you're out. Get on with the game."

"Dad!" Collin jumps up and down on the base, his hands fists. "I was safe. Matt's lying."

"It doesn't matter now. Just pick it up from here." Ed reopens his newspaper to end the discussion.

"No! It's not fair." Collin folds his arms and stands firm on second.

"Fine," Ed says. "If you can't play without arguing, go to your room."

Collin argues a bit more and then stomps to his room.

A moment later, a window squeaks open upstairs. The boys look up to see Collin's bare buttocks smiling at them from the window.

"Come on, Collin!" Matt calls from the stairs. "What are you doing up there?"

"Hurry up!" says Katie. "I want to open my presents!"

Collin is always the last one downstairs on Christmas morning. It isn't that he sleeps late or is slow getting down the stairs. He is right there with Matt and Katie, pouncing on Ed and me in bed—"C'mon, c'mon, hurry up! We need to see if Santa came!"

Pretty much every year, Ed and I stay up until at least three Christmas Eve, wrapping presents and putting together toy kitchens or G.I. Joe headquarters (with their hundreds of stickers). We tell the kids we will take back their toys if they wake us before seven and make them wait upstairs while we turn on the tree lights and get the camera ready for the wow! shot.

In the family room, I line up my camera angle. "Okay!" we call.

"Come on, Collin!" Matt and Katie grouse.

Collin is in his room gathering his presents for all of us. He refuses to come downstairs without them.

"Collin!" Katie says again.

Finally, bare feet thunder down the stairs and across the foyer, and our three children appear in the doorway. Matt is dressed in an Oklahoma University sweatshirt and sweatpants. Katie has on her long Care Bears nightgown. Ten-year-old Collin's dinosaur T-shirt barely covers his underwear. He juggles several hand-wrapped packages, trying not to drop them.

Oohs and aahs follow sharp intakes of breath as the children take in the scene. I click the shutter and Matt and Katie dash to their spots beneath the jeweled tree. Collin comes to Ed and me.

"Here, Mom, this is for you." He hands me a cube wrapped in red with gold stars.

"Here, Dad." He gives his father a long green package.

"Matt," Collin says, presenting his brother a pyramidal silver box.

"Katie, this one's yours." He holds out a present adorned with teddy bears.

"Open them, everybody." Collin smiles and sits in front of me on the floor with one foot tucked under him. His shoulders ripple and he blinks. His knee bounces and his eyes glow as he waits for us to unveil our treasures.

We open our gifts. Mine is a watch with a faceted face and sea-blue band.

"You can add it to your collection," Collin tells me. "Now you have fifteen."

Ed gets a screwdriver. As soon as it is unwrapped, Collin takes it from him and unscrews the handle.

"See, Dad? The other tips are inside. There are two regular and two Phillips heads. That way you don't have to search for the right tool."

Matt's present is a Jose Canseco baseball card.

"I know you've been looking for this one since he made MVP," Collin tells his brother.

Katie unwraps a stuffed animal—a black cat.

"It's to remind you of Princess." Collin's voice is soft. "Doesn't it look just like her? You can pretend she's still alive."

Compliments and thanks and hugs go around, and Collin's eyes light up. Only then does he turn his attention to the pile of presents tagged with his name under the tree.

Collin is so good at selecting gifts that I take him Christmas shopping with me one year to help choose a watch for Ed. The local BJ's Discount Warehouse advertises a great price on one I have my eye on, and Collin agrees it is a terrific choice. We buy the timepiece and then check out the rest of the store. We have never been to a warehouse store—a new concept—before. Collin dances through the aisles.

He revels in the product demonstrations. We sample everything, from Totino's Pizza Rolls to Little Hugs drinks. And of course we need Scotch tape and screwdrivers and copy paper and—"Mom, the Kraft mac and cheese is such a great deal!" We leave, our cart piled high with gadgets and tools and sky-scraping packs of paper towels and toilet paper that take us months to use. The bargain watch has cost a fortune.

Merchandising fascinates Collin. He is entranced by television infomercials and can repeat their shticks, verbatim.

Seeing me sitting at the mirror grousing about blackheads, he says, "Oh, Mom, you should get Proactiv Solution. Two dermatologists developed it. It's powerful to fight acne, but it's also gentle."

I follow his advice and become a Proactiv customer—and an infomercial geek. A night owl, I rack up a surfeit of middle-of-the-night commercials. I order Ginsu knives, weight-loss schemes, probiotics, real estate investment plans, computer software . . .

My husband shakes his head when packages come to the door. "What time did you buy that?" Ed says. "Did Collin talk you into it?"

I sit down at the computer and double-click on Microsoft Word to prepare a worksheet for my third graders. An error message comes on the screen—*not enough memory.*

Huh? Last time I used the computer, there was ample memory.

Collin. He must have changed my settings again to play his games. I click on folders and check the kilobytes reserved by each to find the memory hog. Nothing looks unusual.

Then, as I close *Sim City*, I spy a folder labeled "sexy.jpg." Jpg files are photos—this isn't part of the game. When I double-click, monstrous breasts knock me backward.

I close the picture and check other file folders. Cheerleaders.jpg. Suck.jpg. The further I explore, the more pictures I find, hidden among game files—2chicks.jpg, dirtyone.jpg, pussy.jpg. In all, about a hundred photos and a dozen QuickTime short videos. My hard drive is full of porn!

A generation ago, tween kids stole their dads' *Playboy* magazines or sneaked peeks at naked Africans in *National Geographic*. But in the internet age, kids can indulge prepubescent fantasies with a few clicks. No question who is responsible—Collin and his henchmen, Peter and Jonathan. When I approach Collin about the smut, his eyes fly open as he denies involvement.

"Collin," I say. "I know, without a doubt, it was you."

58

"How?"

"Since I'm a teacher we get our internet service from the state. It has a firewall so students can't access inappropriate material at school. You're the only one here who knows how to circumvent a firewall."

Collin shrugs. A crooked half-smile flashes for an instant, then transforms into a tight-lipped, wide-eyed mask of innocence.

Collin slams the front door and flings his backpack, knocking over a candle on the foyer table.

"Hey!" I shout from the kitchen. "What's going on?" I step into the hallway and unfurl my red cape before a thirteen-year-old raging bull.

"I'm really mad." Collin is breathing hard and his fists are clenched at his sides. "It's those assholes again. I'm going to punch their lights out." He sits down hard on the stair.

"Tell me what happened."

"These kids keep coming up behind me in the hall and smacking me on the back of the head."

"Why?"

"I don't know!" Collin shoots me a look. Stupid mother.

"Did you do something?"

"Nooooo." He rolls his eyes.

"They don't pick on you for no reason."

"Mom! Yes, they do!" Collin insists, hands flying to punctuate. "They call me "retard" and "tic-tac." I can't stand it anymore. If they do it again, that's it."

"What are you planning to do?"

"I'm going to beat the crap out of them." He simulates a right jab.

"Then you'll get into trouble."

He crosses his arms. "I don't care."

"Have you reported them to the principal?"

"She doesn't do anything."

"I just think there must be a better way to handle this."

"Mom, you don't get it!" Collin shakes his head. "I try not to fight and just to ignore it, and then they call me a wimp. I can't keep taking it."

I put my arms around my son. Collin shrugs me off and stomps up the stairs. His door slams and I hear scratchy Nintendo gunshots.

"Fuck!" Collin yells. There is a crash and the gunshots stop.

"Collin, you must need more medicine," I say as I prepare my to-do list. "I haven't refilled your prescriptions in a long while."

"I don't need any," thirteen-year-old Collin says, popping a Hot Pockets into the microwave.

"It's been more than a month. Let me see your bottles."

"I stopped taking it. I don't need it anymore."

"What?" My voice rises. "You're supposed to quit antidepressants gradually. How long since you had your last dose?"

"Couple of weeks now." He bites into the pastry. "I'm good."

I come home to find the kids' report cards on the counter. Katie's is on top. I flip to Matt's, and then to Collin's. "Honor Roll" is stamped in red letters. My hand flies to my heart.

"Collin!" I call. No answer.

I scan the grades. Collin has done well, indeed. It has been a long road, from the achievement test he aced at the end of first grade—every question correct—to this honor roll in eleventh grade. In between, Collin struggled with grades, not because he wasn't brilliant, but because Tourette-associated symptoms of ADHD, depression, and auditory memory difficulties made assignments tedious and difficult to track.

When he was little, he struggled to maintain focus on busywork involving lots of writing. In fourth grade he fell asleep every day during language arts. (When I listened to his teacher drone on at open house, I understood why.) In middle school, if Collin didn't get an assignment written down in the rush at the end of a class, he'd forget about it. Or, he'd do an assignment and forget to turn it in.

I look up as Collin comes in the back door. "Hey, Mom." His standard greeting. He smiles.

I wrap him in a bear hug. "I'm so proud of you," I say, mussing his hair.

Mildly embarrassed, he beams, nods his head, smooths his hair, and grabs a Sprite from the fridge.

"Hey, Mom," Collin says, coming into the family room. He hands me a Best Buy bag.

"What's this?" I ask.

He shrugs and gestures for me to open it. Inside is a CD of Elton John's "Goodbye, England's Rose" eulogy for Princess Diana. I look at Collin with my mouth open, and my smile broadens as I realize what he has done.

"Collin, this is so sweet!"

He smiles. "I know you love Elton John, and you admired Princess Di's charity work. I thought you'd like it."

"I do! Thank you so much!"

When I went through Collin's school backpack after his death, I found his hand-written copy for a radio broadcast on WMCK, McKean High School's radio station. Although he was sports director, Collin also wrote and read headline news at times.

"Good morning, I'm Collin Robinson for WMCK news and here's what's happening—an out-of-control bus veered off I-95 and the edge of an overpass, parents pull seven-year-old out of school because of safety concerns, the Schwartz Center to open in two years after renovations and new additions, University of Delaware is keeping up with technology by spending more on internet and e-mail accounts for students. More details after a word from our sponsors . . ."

III

Five More Days

I hadn't drunk enough of you;
You hadn't tasted enough of life.
There were arguments we needed to have;
Places where we hadn't posed for photos with
you making devil horns behind someone's head;
We had things to begin.

Home Alone

We were home, after what seemed like five years in the hospital. Our pets swarmed us. Maggie and Tigger barked and danced, their claws scratching a snare drum rhythm on the wood floor. Sparckey and White Socks purred as they rubbed up against us, weaving through our legs as if performing in an agility contest. Ed and I slid to the floor, stroking their fur as they covered us in kisses and searched for the reassurance of our scents among all the strange new ones. *Can they smell Collin?* I wondered. *Can they smell death?*

They must have thought we abandoned them. I cried as I hugged Collin's beautiful black cat. *Poor Sparckey—his human will never come home.*

Eventually we disentangled ourselves and stood. Ed refilled the animals' water bowl then sank into a chair in the family room, staring at nothing. I wandered around the first floor, expecting to find everything as we had left it. Ed had stranded dinner on the stove when he rushed out to Collin in the street. The dogs had been shedding bales of fur, and even daily vacuuming was like shoveling snow in a blizzard. Dirty clothes blanketed the laundry room floor, and I couldn't remember when I had last dusted or cleaned the powder room. Not to mention that while Ed and I had stayed in the hospital, the kids and their friends had come home each night. Who knew what food lay moldering in the family room or how tall the piles of dishes would be in the kitchen, stacked precariously on the counter like a Jenga tower built by the Cat in the Hat?

But now—abracadabra!—everything was in its place. Surfaces shone. An image flashed through my mind of Mr. Clean, gold earring agleam, standing with arms crossed, smiling that self-satisfied smile. No, the giant bald guy hadn't visited, but our friends Ethel, Ginny, Joyce, Sandi, and Ann had sneaked in like elves and worked their magic. (Actually, I'm sure they wish they could have snapped their fingers to put everything right. Instead, they must have labored for hours, cleaning and doing laundry.) This was such a blessing. Thankfully, they left Collin's room untouched.

The quiet unnerved me. Our home had buzzed with life—throughout every day, the front door slammed, feet thumped up and down the stairs, music blared, voices rose and fell in laughter or argument, video games beeped and popped, the refrigerator door swooshed open and thunked shut. Now, emptiness echoed.

I found myself on the second floor, with no memory of having climbed the stairs. Resisting the urge to curl up behind the dresses in a corner of my closet, I opened the bathroom window and breathed in the calm of my beloved trees. Silent sentinels, their barren arms reached out to me and we wept together.

I thought I'd feel relief at finally being home. We had left the hospital abruptly. Nurse Pat had said the organ harvesting [ugh!] surgery would take place late that night, and we expected to stay by Collin's side until they wheeled him away. But as before, she banished us to the waiting room. Finally, Ed and I simply showed up at Collin's door, only to be unnerved by the sight of several people in scrubs hovering over his naked body, one rolling an ultrasound transducer over his belly. They told us they would do tests off and on all afternoon to assess the viability of his organs.

The thought of sitting in the waiting room for hours panicked me. I wanted to see my son, but if I couldn't do that, I needed to escape the hospital and the emotions that had bathed my body in cortisol[10] for five days (How was there any left?). None of my composure remained, to be sure. I needed to be where I felt safe and calm.

---

[10] A hormone produced in the adrenal glands that fuels the body's "fight or flight" response.

Although Collin still breathed and his heart beat, he was no longer in that body. "Let's go home," I whispered to Ed. "Can we go home?"

As I leaned on the bathroom windowsill, I bitterly regretted leaving. Perhaps we'd have had a few moments to sit by Collin's side and just drink in his image before it would be forever gone. Wouldn't that have been worth any incarceration in the waiting room? I had thrown away that grace in a weak moment of selfish indulgence.

Now I was safe in my house, but so what? What had I been so eager to get home to? *What is there to do when the world has ended?* There was only the roar of emptiness and grief that shredded my insides with a griffin's talons.

Soft murmurs from downstairs told me the kids and my parents had arrived. I wiped my eyes and went to join them.

The Dying of the Light

I was wrong. There was a lot to do. We had to plan Collin's funeral. Funerals are one of those rituals that bring people together to support and comfort one another. They are also, I suspect, a way to keep the bereaved from lurching from room to room like the living dead or hibernating under the covers until the nightmare ends.

Our first task was to meet with the funeral director. We had been to Doherty's many times for the funerals of relatives and friends, so the Greek Revival building that once seemed imposing had become a place of solace. Red brick promised the strength to carry us and our burdens. Two-story white Doric columns nodded to tradition, that Doherty's century of experience would shepherd us through the process not only competently but with empathy. And the hanging wrought-iron lantern suggested that the light of love infused our painful endeavor. Collin would be honored and we would be cared for.

Inside, the Queen Anne furnishings and Waverly drapes reinforced the message of solid tradition. A grandfather clock hinted that time goes on in the face of death, bonging each milestone to jolt us out of our fog. Despite all this, dread sizzled through me. We were one step closer to the nightmare being real and Collin being gone forever.

My dad had offered to come with Ed and me, and I was grateful to lean on my steadfast anchor. Our family's rock, Dad had accompanied three of his sisters to the funeral home after the deaths of their young husbands. He had coordinated his mother's and father's funerals and the burial of his stillborn son. Later, he said that none of these had been as emotionally staggering as arranging to bury his grandson.

Jim, the funeral director, met us in the vestibule and escorted us to a conference room upstairs. I sat at the large polished wood table between Ed and Dad, the men I loved and trusted most in the world. We agreed to hold a viewing Friday night and the funeral Saturday morning so Collin's classmates and the kids' friends could attend. Next Jim guided us through choices we needed to make—flowers, a guest book, funeral cards, thank you cards, burial vault, limo, pallbearers. Did we want music during the viewing and photos of Collin on display boards? We'd need to meet with the minister and purchase a cemetery plot—Jim would coordinate procedures and timing with both. He explained the procedures for putting an obituary in the newspaper and obtaining death certificates and reminded us to drop off clothes and a photo of Collin to help with their presentation. I told Jim that Collin was naturally pale. "Another mortuary made my great-aunt's face orange," I said, "and I won't be happy if you make my son orange." He promised he would not.

Although Jim was thoroughly professional and compassionate, by this time I was overwhelmed and operated in robot-mode. Every decision felt like another nail in the coffin (which seemed sadly apt) that pushed Collin farther into the ether. My M.O. has always been to be unflappable in a crisis and give in to emotion later, in private, but I was dangerously close to losing it.

Our last task was to choose a casket. We followed Jim into the display room. Ed's knees buckled and I grabbed his arm to steady us both. The dozen or so caskets were artfully displayed, but even so, I shook my head to clear the image of a room filled with vampire coffins from one of Ed's horror movies. The copper and bronze boxes looked elegant, yet cold and industrial. We chose a warm honey oak with cream-colored lining for our horror movie.

Now we had to pay for it all. We drove to the credit union and withdrew all the money in Collin's account. Although I had kept my composure at the funeral home, I broke down as I explained to the clerk that this had been Collin's college fund, money we had been saving since he was a baby, and we were now using it to bury him.

We had endured a five-day vigil at the hospital, hoping against hope for a miracle. Now we would wait five days at home, the "thing with feathers"[11] having flown the coop, knowing that after the fifth day we would never again see or touch our son. Sitting alone with such thoughts was agonizing, but our family and friends came to help shoulder the burden. Those closest to us arrived shortly after we got home from the hospital. Others dropped in and out all week or called to check on us. I don't remember anything anyone said, but I remember that they showed up for us, sat with us, hugged us, listened to us, cried with us. And they took over running our household—vacuuming up the doggie tumbleweeds, cleaning the powder room, answering the phone, preparing meals—everyday chores that become Herculean tasks to those from whom grief exacts a toll just to turn over in bed.

Everyone brought food. Sandwiches, subs, and chicken salad, along with salads, chips, and sodas kept our visitors fed. We grazed on cake, brownies, doughnuts, chocolate-covered pretzels, cookies. Fruit and cheese baskets and veggie trays helped us resist the carb roller coaster of energy and ennui. Casseroles of delicious lasagna, spaghetti, chicken tetrazzini, ziti, chili, meatballs, and chicken and dumplings were a blessing at dinnertime. Several people even sent us breakfast.

These offerings put the comfort in comfort food. But the tradition of bringing food during mourning is not simply about being kind or sparing the bereaved the work of cooking. Sharing food, commenting on how delicious it was, provided respites from sitting silently, impotently, staring sightlessly at one another, wishing the floor would crack open and swallow us. And science tells us that eating satisfying food prompts the brain to release endorphins, which buoy mood and induce feelings of calm, which we desperately needed.

I threw myself into funeral preparations as if planning a wedding, determined that everything be perfect to honor Collin. Everyone helped. Matt prepared a music tape to play during the viewing. My aunts and cousins offered suggestions for songs and readings. My

---

[11] "Hope" is the thing with feathers - / That perches in the soul - / And sings the tune without the words - / And never stops - at all – —Emily Dickinson

sister-in-law Marybeth took Katie shopping for a new dress and shoes and bought Collin new khakis and a royal blue Henley shirt, along with underwear and socks. We put Collin's clothes into a paper bag to take to Doherty's. Later, it occurred to me that the last two items probably went unused.

Katie and my friend Kathy helped me comb through photo albums to select pictures for a photo board. There was baby Collin, splashing and smiling in his bath in the kitchen sink. Toddler Collin, blond curls bouncing in the breeze as he was pushed in his swing. Collin with a ten-foot boa constrictor around his neck at his Jungle John eighth birthday party. Collin in his baseball uniform; riding his new bike; sitting at the computer. Every scene evoked a memory, and seeing my distress, the girls offered to finish without me. But excruciating as it was, the memories wrapped themselves around me, keeping me from disintegrating into dust.

Funeral Fugue

We would hold Collin's funeral at St. Mark's United Methodist Church. My mother had been the choir director there for decades, and the music had lured us in and the members had adopted us as family. Rev. Ellis asked for memories of Collin he could share during the funeral, so before Ed and I met with him, our family sat together and reminisced. Smiles crept out for the first time since the accident, and laughter snuck through the house. As you find the stories throughout this book, you'll understand.

I worried that the pastor might object to our secular musical selections, but he graciously agreed to all our requests, including the plan for my big Catholic family to process into the sanctuary behind Collin's casket, rather than having it already in place when people arrived, in the Methodist way. He walked Ed and me through the service and wrote down our Collin stories.

Everything was set, and we steeled ourselves for the wretched weekend ahead—the knockout punch of viewing and funeral. It was something we had to do for Collin, and we would do it.

When I awoke on Friday, my body buzzed as if a million bees were trying to escape. Every sensory input sent them into a stinging frenzy. The pain ratcheted up as the day progressed. Perhaps we all felt that way, or maybe Ed, Matt, and Katie followed my lead through uncharted territory. We spun individual cocoons and spent the day in a sort of communal somnambulistic state, shutting out the world and our own thoughts. I dressed for the viewing robotically, in slow motion, as if some alchemy of grief had turned my bones to lead.

No one spoke as we drove the three miles to the funeral home, a ride my friend Kelly likens to "going to a Nazi death camp." Every bump in the road cried out, "Collin. Collin. Collin."

Seeing Collin quickened my heart and exploded it at the same time. For a moment I just drank in his beautiful face. Then, like I had checked my newborn's fingers and toes, I surveyed every detail. He looked pale (not orange!), as normal, but gave no hint of his usual shy smile. His eyelids were sunken, which dismayed me, as the organ donation representative had promised us the surgeon would insert artificial orbs after removing Collin's eyes, his kind eyes. The terror I felt when we agreed to donate Collin's organs sizzled through me like a specter. Deep breaths calmed my shaking.

I stroked my son's cheek. Collin's once baby-soft skin was cold and stiff, the tissue beneath hard, petrified. I was a different kind of petrified. Although I had touched embalmed loved ones before, most had been elderly. It felt wrong for my vibrant child to feel this way. And he was unnaturally still. In the hospital, Collin lay relaxed with no tics. But his heart beat a determined rhythm, and his chest, a slave to the respirator, rose and fell, rose and fell.

Now, nothing. He would never again wave his hands wildly to punctuate a point. Never throw back his head and show all his perfect teeth in a gleeful laugh. Never thump downstairs on Christmas morning, his arms overflowing with gifts. Never grind his feet into the dirt to bat or run the bases. He would never wrap his arms around a soulmate or cradle his own baby. I wondered which pain was worse—my grief at what happened or the pain of what never will.

The horror continued as I touched Collin's chest and it crinkled. Beneath his signature Henley and khakis, his torso was swathed in plastic to keep fluids from leaking out. I gasped and Ed broke into tears, and we rocked together for a long moment. One more indignity for Collin, one more kick in the gut for us. Collin chose to donate his organs, and we supported that, but our brains had been seared with an image of our beautiful boy as a shell, his organs "harvested," his eyes missing, wrapped in a garbage bag for all eternity.

Finally I broke away and reached for the paper bag I had brought. Collin's spirit had left us in the hospital, but his body was still in that casket—all alone. I needed to comfort my son, to surround him with familiar things. I needed to see him in my mind alive and whole, if only for a moment. I had collected the stuffed duckie he had loved as a toddler and somehow never threw out, a few G.I. Joe vehicles and Matchbox cars, his car keys, his class ring, a laser disc video game, his McKean High School baseball cap, and some baseball cards. Matt contributed his own number 34 McKean varsity baseball shirt. I busied myself arranging Collin's treasures around him, enveloping him in life and love. Visitors would envision him exuberant, racing Matchbox cars, trading baseball cards, playing video games. He would stay vital just a bit longer.

Ed's and my parents and siblings joined us for a few private moments with Collin. Then the grandfather clock chimed, and it was time to open the doors. I positioned myself where I could see Collin, painfully aware that the window to do so was quickly slipping closed. Ed, Matt, Katie, and our parents lined up next to me. Boxes of tissues were within reach. The lights were bright, and Michael Jackson's "Never Can Say Goodbye" drifted from the speakers. I would catch other lyrics and riffs off and on through the evening.

Friends and family, coworkers and neighbors, and people we hadn't seen in years poured in and kept coming for the next four hours. Even the ambulance attendants who transported Collin to the hospital came. Everyone waited patiently in a very long line to offer comfort and support. Their outpouring of love and concern was not just sympathy and platitudes. Instead, we felt the physical energy of love envelop us as our loved ones hugged us and we cried together. I felt almost giddy as we celebrated Collin, as if we were warding off the reaper for a few hours. We left the funeral home that night exhausted but uplifted, knowing how many people loved us and how many lives Collin had touched. Yet another blessing waited at home—my fellow teachers had prepared us a delicious buffet.

Funeral rituals can be difficult—excruciating, even—and sometimes people wonder why anyone endures them. No one wants to cry or feel miserable, so the trend nowadays is toward quickie visitations immediately before a funeral or doing away with the viewing altogether. But mourning rituals are adaptive, having evolved to shepherd us through the morass of anguish and provide an opportunity for empathy. Most of all, they keep us from flailing alone in our darkest hours. Every touch and embrace, every pained smile, every murmured condolence was precious air that kept us from drowning.

Even tears were blessed gifts. As author and diplomat Washington Irving, who mourned a fiancée and a brother, wrote, "There is a sacredness in tears. They are not the mark of weakness, but of power. They speak more eloquently than ten thousand tongues. They are the messengers of overwhelming grief, of deep contrition, and of unspeakable love." As difficult as it was, Collin's viewing helped us realize we would not grieve alone.

Saturday dawned angry, as storm clouds gathered like horses giddy for battle, the wind whipping them into a frenzy. The weather mirrored my emotions. There was no turning back—no way to claim a headache or postpone until next Tuesday. Collin's accident had brought our lives to a halt, and his death ended the world as we knew it. Now his funeral would thrust us into a future we neither anticipated nor wanted. As I dressed, I steeled myself for the long, agonizing day of tears ahead.

Once again, we were silent on the way to Doherty's, as we passed people walking their dogs, going to the Acme, getting gas. . . . Poet Robert Frost, who buried four of his six children, remarked on this cruel irony: "In three words I can sum up everything I've learned about life: it goes on."

In the parking lot, we sat in the car a long moment, our refusal to cooperate one last poetic protest—"Rage, rage against the dying of the light."[12] Finally we dragged ourselves inside. Our parents, siblings, cousins, aunts and uncles, nieces and nephews greeted us with hugs, tears already glistening. They said their goodbyes to Collin, and then Ed, Matt, Katie, and I went in to see him. Standing by the casket, we wrapped our arms around one another and sobbed, each whispering our own messages to Collin.

---

[12] Dylan Thomas, "Do Not Go Gentle into That Good Night."

Jim came in and told us it was time to go to the church. We removed Collin's belongings from the casket, leaving just a few meaningful items. I slid his class ring onto my finger and clutched Duckie. We took one last, long look at Collin, then Jim closed the lid forever on our beautiful boy. It felt like a punch in the gut.

The pallbearers—Collin's cousins, Richie, Mark, Paul, and Hunter; and his friends, Giancarlo, Peter, Jonathan, Chuck, and Patrick—loaded the casket into the hearse. Stoic, they acted out a scene no one should ever have to perform.

Beams, walls, and pews of stained wood lend a beautiful warmth to the St. Mark's sanctuary. Jewel-toned stained-glass windows line the room's left side and fill the soaring space above the doors from the narthex, and when the sun streams in, the effect is heavenly. This day though, the sun played truant. My mind elsewhere, I might not have noticed if everything had been painted purple with green spots. What did break through my fog was sweet perfume that wafted from the funeral flowers on the altar. It circulated, touching everyone in turn, connecting us.

But the best thing about St. Mark's has always been its music, always able to reach me even when I occasionally rolled my eyes during the sermon. As our family processed in behind Collin's casket, "How Great Thou Art" thundered from the pipe organ and hundreds of voices harmonized. My heart skipped a beat.

After everyone sat down, you could have heard a mouse breathe. Rev. Baker said a prayer. He had co-officiated at Ed's and my wedding and baptized Collin and Katie. Next he read from scripture—Psalm 27 ("The Lord is my light and my salvation; whom shall I fear?"), St. John 14 (Let not your heart be troubled: ye believe in God, believe also in me. In my Father's house are many mansions: if it were not so, I would have told you. I go to prepare a place for you."), and Romans 8 ("For I am persuaded, that neither death, nor life, nor angels, nor principalities, nor powers, nor things present, nor things to come, Nor height, nor depth, nor any other creature, shall be able to separate us from the love of God, which is in Christ Jesus our Lord.").

Our friend Bert sang John Lennon's "Beautiful Boy," ending with the whisper, "Beautiful Collin." I just let the tears run down my face. More prayers, then Bert lent his flawless tenor to Eric Clapton's "Tears in Heaven." Next Rev. Ellis read one of my favorite verses, from Ecclesiastes 3 ("To everything there is a season, and a time to every purpose under heaven: A time to be born, and a time to die . . .").

The reverend let the sobs and honks subside, then stepped to the pulpit. He talked about God, and heaven, and everlasting life, and then related several of our Collin stories. He asked if anyone else wanted to share anything, and my brother stepped up.

Among the stories Jeff told was the time he had taken Collin to an Orioles baseball game at Memorial Stadium. Although Collin loved baseball, the food court was more fascinating that day, and he capitalized on his uncle's largesse and inexperience (Jeff was not yet a father) to wheedle dollar after dollar. They were seated in the center of a long row of bleachers in the outfield. Collin climbed in and out a dozen times, getting a soda, pretzel, hot dogs, ice cream, popcorn. . . . By game's end, Jeff said, Collin had no clue about the score but was on a first-name basis with everyone in the row.

Collin's godfather, our former neighbor Rich, also shared his favorite Collin stories. My favorite was of the day in mid-summer when Collin convinced the former New Yorker to bring a hermit crab home from the beach—an hour-and-a-half drive. Familiar with the crustaceans, the Delaware congregation groaned, imagining the stench in that hot car. Collin was lucky he made it home that night. The crab did not, although its spirit lingered on for weeks.

Ed's dad reminisced about times he and Ed's mom had babysat Collin. He was impressed at how much Collin knew about everything, including the latest Phillies score. He spoke for a few minutes, then broke down in tears.

I had messed up big time when it came to Collin's eulogy. My dad had always been the one we called on to do difficult things, but because I thought it might be too painful for him, I asked my brother and Collin's godfather to eulogize our son. My sister was terribly hurt, as she was Collin's godmother and had been close to him. I wanted to slide under the rug—of course, Kelly was the perfect choice. In my shock, I operated on autopilot and sought someone who would be a rock, like my dad—so I only considered a man. It went against all my feminist tendencies and didn't even make logical sense, as I had delivered several eulogies myself. When I realized what I had done, I begged Kelly to speak too, and for Collin, she agreed.

Kelly's remembrance took a different tack. She modeled her remarks on *Everything I Ever Needed to Know I Learned in Kindergarten* by Robert Fulghum. "Just Do It! All I Needed to Know I Learned from Collin Robinson" dispensed wisdom and lessons gleaned from the boy who was full of life. "Smile with your whole face and light up the entire room," she said. "Play baseball, but take time out to pick the flowers and dig in the dirt in the outfield if you feel like it. . . . Wear shorts in January just for fun. . . . Become an expert at everything . . ."

The stories went on for a long time, and we all found ourselves laughing instead of crying. The mood carried over into the next hymn, "Blessed Assurance."

But the tears were fated to return. Bert's final solo, "Forever Young" by Rod Stewart, defied anyone to remain dry-eyed. Rev. Ellis offered a blessing, then Collin's boys took their places alongside the casket. We followed them down the aisle singing a St. Mark's favorite, "On Eagles' Wings" by Michael Joncas. As we recessed, we came face to face with the congregation. Unlike at a normal church service, I knew every face. Here were my cousins, there an aunt. Over there I saw neighbors, and a few pews later Collin's friends from high school. Many wiped their eyes, but everyone smiled as best they could, sending the message of their solidarity with our pain. Eventually too many tears blurred my vision and I let Ed lead me, blind, the rest of the way. At the curb, Jim removed and folded the linen pall that covered Collin's casket and the bearers loaded it into the hearse.

It was over. We had survived the funeral. It had been exquisite, reflecting both our heartbreak and our love and reminding everyone of the impact Collin had had on all our lives. Later, many people commented on it personally or in their remarks on sympathy cards. My friend Lee who had known third-grade Collin wrote, "The service for Collin was *tender*" [her italics]— the perfect characterization.

Of course, the day was far from over. I had mixed feelings— wanting it to end so I could be alone with my grief; wanting it to go on forever so Collin wouldn't truly be gone.

We followed the hearse to the cemetery, lights flashing. All Saints is a serene yet comfortable place, with gently rolling grassy fields dotted with mature trees. My grandparents, uncles, and baby brother were buried there. We had chosen plots in the "Pure of Heart" section, watched over by larger-than-life bronze statues of St. Stanislaus Kostka, St. Maria Goretti, and Kateri Tekakwitha. Collin's grave was to be between Ed's and mine, just down the hill from the local Catholic high school. We could hear the pings of aluminum bats smacking balls as the baseball team practiced. We thought Collin would appreciate that.

The site was ready—a half-dozen chairs lined up on green AstroTurf to prevent muddy shoes, brass railings to keep anyone from falling in, the excavated dirt covered discreetly some distance away. An awning sheltered the grave and mourners from the elements. The pallbearers brought Collin's casket to the grave and the funeral directors encircled it with flower arrangements. These had filled the funeral home at the viewing. Many had been transported to the church for the funeral and then brought to the cemetery. Later we would take a few home with us. The remaining bouquets would be sent to the hospital.

Even on this gloomy day, the flowers broadcast beauty. Part of their allure is that they sprout and blossom, spread their radiance, and then, before we can become blasé, disappear. Collin's life had that same ephemeral beauty. But his was not just physical appeal, rather the Platonic ideal of beauty encompassing integrity and goodness—"The good is the beautiful."

Unfortunately, the weather cried ugly. Before Rev. Ellis could begin, the skies opened. It was as if heaven were sobbing over our loss. Or maybe Collin was pranking us. I asked everyone to squeeze together beneath the meager awning so more people could take cover, but many more remained out in the open, some with umbrellas, others getting soaked. I never made it to a chair, instead crushed among damp wool coats, unable to see anything. However, the service was short and people hurried back to their cars, letting us linger to add flowers atop the casket and have a private moment with Collin.

I couldn't bring myself to say goodbye. A funeral and burial are as final as things get, but to say goodbye felt like severing our connection, as if an oak had toppled in a storm and cut the phone line.

Maybe it was magical thinking, but I wanted—fully expected—to maintain our bond beyond the ether, if only in my hopes and dreams. So instead of saying goodbye, I told Collin I loved him and missed him already. I asked him to send me signs that he was with me. *Someday, Collin,* I said silently, *we'll be together again and tell each other all our stories.*

We visited our other loved ones' graves before leaving All Saints, so when we got back home, the house was already packed with people. Bizarrely, it reminded me of the Royal Exchange, a local nightclub Ed and I had visited a few times in our twenties, where bodies were packed so tightly that a trip to the bathroom involved intimate contact with dozens of people. Happier times—when unlimited possibilities lay ahead. But as Lady Mary Crawley said in *Downton Abbey*, "Everything seems so golden one moment then turns to ashes the next."

The mood was subdued, but not somber. I tried to speak with as many people as I could. Everyone hugged us and expressed their condolences. They told us the service was lovely and shared stories about Collin. There was good food, courtesy of the St. Mark's choir.

After an hour or so, the sensory input overwhelmed me, and I pushed and squeezed my way through the crowd to the powder room. It was a relief to let my smile thaw and breathe for a moment. It wasn't that I didn't want everyone there—I was terrified at the thought of them leaving. For the past week, I had been play-acting, following an unwritten script. I knew that once the rituals were complete and silence stalked the house, reality would swoop in and remind us that this was no play, or even a nightmare we'd wake up from.

We'd be alone in the stillness.

I already knew I couldn't stop time, and one by one, people said their goodbyes and the house was quiet. I sank into the couch and just sat, not moving, not talking, not seeing.

Collin was gone forever.

Visceral Rhetoric

*G*rief is not merely sadness. It is pain—physical pain. Ninja-nimble, grief may pop up as headache, stomachache, backache. It is both tick and host, swelling to bursting and being sucked dry. It is a newborn with day and night mixed up; an outlaw whose big guns are loaded with heart attack, stroke, and cancer. Grief's favorite mask is depression—stress, its ever-present Tonto.

Anne K. Finkbeiner, a science journalist, described her grief over her son's death: "The pain is actually physical, mostly in your stomach and chest. Your chest feels crushed and you can't seem to catch your breath. I remember feeling pinned like a butterfly, or somehow eviscerated." The mood lasts not a moment, or a day, but months, years, and molests will and energy. It slinks backward in time, as well, thrusting into memory until it seems things were always so. Did we really have him? Or was it a dream?

Questions become action verbs. Why did he have to die? Does he still exist in the ether, and can he see me? How can I believe in a loving God who turns a blind eye to torment? Is there logic and meaning to life or are we bacteria in the gut of a soulless bio-machine? I pummel my fists against the useless quest. There are no answers, nor will there ever be. Still, I am unable to stop.

"Give sorrow words," wrote William Shakespeare in *Macbeth*. "The grief that does not speak / Whispers the o'er-fraught heart and bids it break." But words, like other friends—not up to the task—desert me. Anguish, misery, agony, suffering, fear, torment are strings of letters devoid of passion. There are no words for pain, said surgeon-cum-author Richard Selzer, only metaphor. The same is true of grief—its rhetoric is not literary, but visceral.

The sensation is real, but you are as in a dream and don't know to will yourself to wake. A giant mirror reflects a visage you barely recognize, a hollow skull with glass eyes and no mouth. Others surround you, but you are alone, which both satisfies and infuriates you. All around is colorless vacuum, with relief a silvery glow in the distance—a mile, ten, a hundred? You slog, as if dragging cement overshoes through wet sand, but make no headway. The glow morphs into a hulking, electric cloud that pulls terror, inch by inch like an acid tapeworm, from your throat until your guts spill around you. Your silent scream is not human. You die, and then gather what you can of yourself, leaving a good portion coated with sand like so much cat shit, and trudge on, diminished; no heartbeat.

You exhale, wanting to crumple into forever sleep, the dreamless kind, but cannot break the promises you made to people you don't remember. The glow reappears, and you reach it this time, only to have it dissolve in laughter and pelt you with crystal slivers that lodge in your eyes. Then the tape plays over again, and again, and again, until you seize awake—and realize you had not been asleep.

IV
The New Abnormal

Night . . .
Reality rests its swollen eyes
as I strip off the day's costume,
scrub the smile that veils my eyes,
relieve anguish of its tender corset and
stand my grief bare-naked and honest.

An Unexpected Taskmaster

Many people think the funeral is the hardest moment for bereaved parents. But we were to learn that finding a way to cope with the forever absence of our child is much worse. I was numb, floating in a bubble, the world around me a hazy video. I wanted to crawl beneath a pile of blankets and curl into a ball like a hedgehog, my spines warding off the outside world, and never leave my bed again. A modern Frankenstein's monster, I had died, the new me an assemblage of disparate parts awaiting a spark of reanimation. None came. I couldn't focus to read or write. Even TV, the ultimate passive pursuit, overwhelmed. Huge swaths of content passed by unnoticed, and the parts that did register didn't make sense. Usually I couldn't have told you what show was on. Watching a comedy was like being stabbed repeatedly—how could anyone brazen to laugh when Collin was dead? Worse, I discovered the unwritten rule that all TV shows and movies must include a death, an accident, or someone bouncing off a car's hood.

Ed tried to console me, to hold me—to fix things for me. I wanted none of it. He couldn't bring Collin back. He wanted me to console him, to hold him, but I couldn't bear it. Once high school sweethearts, we devolved into roommates—sharing meals, sitting on the couch together, and sleeping in the same bed—but grieving alone and lonely. It was several years before I was once again able to reach out to my love and let him in.

I would have liked to shut myself up in a tower à la Rapunzel or get in the car and drive—and drive and drive. . . . Adopt a new identity and pretend my previous life had been a dream. But life is relentless. Ed backed off when I asked, but reality laughed when I tried to push it away. The ultimate perpetual motion machine, it insisted that I keep up and found task after task for me to do.

Since I was too shell-shocked to return to my teaching job, I needed to apply for disability. I had paid into disability insurance for years, and now that I needed it, they made it as difficult as possible to obtain. The application form asked for detailed descriptions of symptoms, dates, ID numbers, and the like. At a time when I could barely speak a coherent sentence, struggled to comprehend anything I read, and had trouble generating the energy to turn over in bed, I had to search for the necessary documents and fashion a coherent narrative. Even with my dad's help, what might previously have taken an hour or two to complete took days, as I did a little at a time and stopped when I became overwhelmed.

We also needed to purchase a headstone for the cemetery and decided on a single one to cover (literally) Collin, Ed, and me. Connie at Cecil Memorials helped us create a design that reflected who we are. We put ROBINSON in large Roman letters in the center. To honor Collin's interest in computers, we put his name and dates in the screen of a stylized computer. This turned out beautifully—if you didn't know it was a computer, you might just see a marquee with steps below, which also framed Collin's ESPN dream. Someday Ed's and my names and dates will flank Collin's. The Catholic cemetery required a religious symbol on every stone, so in the top right corner, we chose a Celtic cross to honor our Irish heritage. In the top left corner, we created a scene to document our collective passions— under our dogwood tree (the stonemason made it an oak, which was fine) a baseball and bat for Ed and Collin, a book for Collin and me, musical notes for Ed and me, dog and cat footprints for all of us. Around the perimeter, we put the line from Shakespeare's *Romeo and Juliet* that we had adopted as our tribute to Collin: "When he shall die, take him and cut him out in little stars, and he will make the face of heaven so fine that all the world will be in love with night and pay no worship to the garish sun."

Like the viewing, funeral, and burial, designing Collin's headstone was another step in recognizing the finality of his death. Memorial stones are made of granite or bronze because those materials hold up to the weather. But they also carry symbolic meaning. The installation of the heavy slab was like sealing shut a door to Collin, never to be opened again. I got through it the same way I had the other steps—by making sure it was exceptional to reflect and honor my extraordinary son.

We selected a peach and gray speckled granite for the stone. What arrived from the quarry was orange and black. Although Halloween was one of Collin's favorite holidays, I shuddered when I saw the garish thing. Cecil replaced the stone.

Months later, I met a woman at the cemetery. She said she and her husband visited loved ones regularly and always stopped at Collin's grave because they thought his memorial was so unique and meaningful.

Although mind-clouds made mundane activities difficult, as long as I looked at tasks as tributes to Collin, I found that I could mask my grief and plow through them. I held the monster at bay the way Collin suppressed his tics for a short time. My friend and Collin's guidance counselor, Vicki, told me that several students with TS frequently ate lunch with her. "It's an explosion of tics," she said. "I see them in the classroom with hardly a movement. But over lunch in my office, they talk and laugh, tics firing all over the room like it's the Fourth of July." When she asked them about it, Collin explained: "A tic is like a fart. There are places it's not polite to let it out, so you try to hold it. Other places, it's okay, so you let it rip. Here, it's safe."

I could hold my grief like a fart for a little while to accomplish something for Collin. My next job was a true labor of love.

In the hospital and continuing through (and even after) the funeral, many people had blessed us with their presence, words of support, and acts of love. I wanted them to know that their kindness had kept us from giving up. Thank-you cards emblazoned with a Celtic cross had been part of our funeral package, but I wanted something more personalized. I designed cards featuring the quotation from *Romeo and Juliet*. In the top left corner, I watercolored a swash of night sky and punched out five tiny stars to represent our family. I wrote an individual note in each. It took me several months to complete all the thank yous, including letters to the hospital, doctors, nurses, and ambulance attendants.

Collin couldn't ward off his tics forever, and eventually I ran out of projects. An avalanche of grief buried me. Pick a metaphor, and I felt it—a tidal wave drowning me, a boulder crushing me, a parasite eating me from the inside out, falling into a bottomless hole with spikes along the sides, having died but they forgot to bury me. I slept most of the day, leaving my bed only to go to the cemetery or have dinner with my family. At night, as I tossed awake, my thoughts tumbled and convulsed like cotton shirts in a dryer that come out wrinkled, their collars creased and sleeves twisted into ropes.

In Collin's Room

One day I wandered into Collin's room and stayed. I curled up in his bed and turned my face to the wall like author Frank McCourt's mother after the successive deaths of three of her children. I had sobbed when I first read the passage in *Angela's Ashes*, but now I had a grim new appreciation of what she endured. Sometimes blocking everything out is all you can do. I usually got up late, went to the cemetery, and spent a few hours in Collin's room. Ding! Dinnertime.

Collin's sheets and pillow hoarded his scent. I nestled into memories—the faint musk that marked his entrance into puberty; the sweet child's sweat as he hugged me after a backyard game of baseball; the baby powder softness of his head as infant Collin snuggled, asleep in my arms.

A paper bag in my closet held the clothes Collin wore the day of his accident—the clothes the ambulance attendants had cut off him. Sometimes I took them out and smothered myself in Collin's fear and blood, wishing those could have been mine instead of his. I should have moved them into a plastic bag because over time, the brown paper bag smell overwhelmed everything else. The day I lost Collin's scent was the day I lost my son all over again.

Collin's room was a mess. It had been a mess his whole life, and the objects shifted from one place to another like sand dunes. He was too busy playing, learning, and creating to tidy up, almost as if he knew such a chore was a waste of precious life. Insisting that he clean his room triggered countless meltdowns. Eventually I stopped insisting. Now I was glad, as I saw him everywhere I looked.

Draped over the back of his desk chair was his red satin jacket with "Phillies" written in white across the chest. On his desk lay a binder of plastic pages that held his favorite baseball cards. The shelves held rocks and minerals, cat tchotchkes, baseball action figures, and "valuable" baseball cards in Plexiglas blocks. A low bookshelf held a full set of *World Book,* along with dozens of other books, old favorites *Sharks* and *Scary Stories to Tell in the Dark* lined up with newer ones like *The Outsiders* and *Roll of Thunder, Hear My Cry.* Collin had recommended the latter as a story I would enjoy. I cried as I realized I had never taken his advice.

Old sneakers, dirty and smelly, one lace broken, had been pushed far under the bed, along with several unopened cans of Dr. Pepper, Micro Machines camo vehicles, building blocks, assorted markers, Duckie, video game flowcharts, sketches of futuristic military vehicles, and pages of video game "cheat" codes in Collin's handwriting.

A chest held childhood toys he hadn't touched in years—bulldozers, front-end loaders, and dump trucks; Matchbox cars; Construx; Transformers; G.I. Joe vehicles and action figures. Now the chest served as a table for Collin's TV and stereo, with a Nintendo console, controllers, and game cartridges scattered around it on the floor. I could pretend Collin would saunter in at any minute and the beeps and pops of *Mario Kart* would fill the air.

I navigated the red, white, blue, and gray Lego mines that spotted the carpet along with scraps of notebook paper, playing cards, empty cups, and issues of *National Geographic.* Here and there I found feathers, even though Collin did not have a feather pillow. All of us found feathers in our paths at regular intervals, usually just as we thought of Collin, and we decided they were his way of saying hi.

Collin's dresser was the most organized surface in the room. A *Mortal Combat* videodisc stood on end next to a half-empty Toblerone (his favorite candy); a cartoon of Cartman from *South Park,* his comb, suede brush, Chap-Stik, and a new toothbrush were arrayed in front of them. Collin's wallet, car keys, and class ring rested in front of his clock radio, waiting to be grabbed on his way out the door.

Seeing and touching the objects Collin had touched kept me connected with him, as if they retained some of his essence, his energy. Even as I sobbed, the memories were a comfort. After nearly a year, the clutter finally got to me and I cleaned up his room. It brought a new sense of calm, but sometimes I regretted it, as I lost a bit more of my son.

In the beginning, sensory stimulation was like knives stabbing me, and I preferred stillness and quiet. In Collin's room, I disappeared into a safe (ha!) little world in which I was in control (haha!). No one made any demands on me and time was meaningless. Sometimes I slept. Sometimes I lay awake while my mind drifted, my thoughts tumbling in a sort of a waking dream state. Some days I looked out the window at the trees. A lot of the time I cried. One evening I simply screamed out my anguish at the top of my lungs. My daily to-do list:

1) get up,
2) survive,
3) go back to bed.

That was all I could manage. I took heart in artist and author Yumi Sakugawa's words: "Sometimes it's okay if the only thing you did today was breathe."

Eventually I began listening to Collin's music while I sat in his room. Matt made me a mix tape of the Dave Matthews Band and Collin's other favorite songs and artists, and I played it over and over, disappearing into the sound and looking for meaning (and messages from Collin, I admit) in the lyrics. I learned all the words.

My student Kimberly's family sent me a blank journal, but I had put it aside, unable to focus enough to string words together. It whispered to me from the counter though, and one day I picked it up, took it to Collin's room, and began to fill it with tears, anger, desperation, and questions—so many questions. *Why did this happen? Is there anyone up there in charge? Where is Collin now? Who am I now?* Over the next several years, I filled more than a dozen such books.

Sometimes, though, prose can't fully express intense, complex emotions. As poet Audre Lorde wrote, "Poetry is the way we help give name to the nameless so it can be thought." So one day while I sat on Collin's bed, I put my pain into a very bad poem. My only previous experiences with poetry were high school and college

93

literature courses and the humorous jingles I had composed as a child for homemade Mother's and Father's Day cards. Still, I persevered, writing dozens of poems over many months. A few years later, when I was hired to teach a college course in creative writing, I gave myself a crash course in poetry. With a new understanding of the importance of action verbs, imagery, sensory details, sound, metaphor, and symbolism, I revised my poems. Periodically, I continue to revisit them. Snippets of these poems begin each chapter of this book.

I also began reading again, holed up in Collin's room. A voracious reader all my life, I had been frustrated not to be able to enjoy books after Collin died. Like my inability to focus on TV, I had trouble tracking lines of text, as if I had suddenly developed dyslexia. Finishing a paragraph, I'd have no idea what I just read or even remember what book I had open in my lap. After about a year, though, the fog lifted and I devoured books on the topics that consumed me—what happens after we die, dealing with grief, the nature of God, spirituality. Reading again was a blessing that provided many hours of escape from the all-consuming pain of real life and the mundane responsibilities that threatened to push me over the edge.

Tiptoeing Out

*L*ong before the COVID-19 pandemic, I self-quarantined because of grief. Interacting with others was exhausting, so I rarely left the house. We didn't go out to eat, and after I broke down in the greeting card aisle at K-Mart, I did no more shopping. When I did leave the house, it was usually to visit the cemetery. Just through the entry gate, my car always lurched and thumped through a deep, uneven gully in the pavement. There was no way around the bump. It made me imagine I was tossing in the current as I crossed the river Styx.[13] Around the curve and a left turn and I was "at Collin's."

I arranged fresh flowers in the vase at the foot of the headstone. The deer ate them at dusk and I brought another meal the next day. They liked tulips the best. Some visitors opted for artificial flowers, but I held out for several years, imagining the does bringing their fawns to have dinner with Collin.

The cemetery was beautiful and peaceful, and a stiff wind nearly always swept down the hill from the high school and found its legs as it galloped across the grassy field. Crows laughed at my grief, and I understood why, as a boy, author Frank McCourt threw stones at

---

[13] In Greek mythology, the River Styx was the border between the world and the underworld.

them during his brother Oliver's burial.[14] Geese glided down to the nearby pond, going about the business of living, oblivious to the thousands of crypts filled with death lined in rows beneath the deceptive blanket of green. And over it all, to crib from C. S. Lewis, "[Collin's] absence [was] like the sky, spread over everything."

As I sat on the grass by Collin's grave, I talked to my son, cried, ranted, pulled weeds, recited the Shakespeare quotation on the stone. Often, another mother sat at her son's grave a few feet away, reading aloud. We never spoke, and I never saw her look up, each of us consumed by her own calamity.

Besides going to the cemetery, I also visited two of my favorite aunts. Although I had lots of family and friends to talk to, there was something extra comforting about sharing my feelings with people who "got" it, who knew what it was like to have your entire world burn down. My dad's sister Sally's husband had been murdered at age twenty-eight. A Delaware State Police detective, Uncle Bob was investigating a burglary in progress at a local motel where three men were stealing televisions. One approached Uncle Bob's car and shot him in the face and chest with a sawed-off shotgun. Left with two girls, three and seven, Aunt Sal never got over the tragedy. She never dated, stayed at home except for family gatherings, and stopped driving once her daughter got her license.

Diagnosed with breast cancer before Collin died, Aunt Sal had a unique perspective—she had experienced great loss and faced her own mortality. We talked about Collin and Uncle Bob and about death and living. She showed me a letter I had sent her one year on the anniversary of Uncle Bob's death, in which I told her how profoundly it had affected me and how much I missed him and loved her. She had kept the letter in a drawer in her buffet table for decades.

She returned the favor, writing Ed and me a long letter after Collin died. (In fact, all three of my widowed aunts wrote us letters.) She remembered his smile as he played with her grandsons Paul and Hunter and how he "expressed himself and his opinions so

---

[14] Frank McCourt, *Angela's Ashes.*

96

eloquently." She warned me that Ed and I would "be lonely in a crowd and feel terrible on a bright and sunny day."

Aunt Sal had been a teacher and enjoyed discussing the books I was reading about grief and what happens when you die. We debated God and religion and considered the impact of our Irish Catholic background. She often wore a sweatshirt with a quotation attributed to Irish poet W. B. Yeats: "Being Irish, he had an abiding sense of tragedy, which sustained him through temporary periods of joy." "Our family is like the Kennedys," Aunt Sal said. "We've both experienced so much tragedy." Sometimes we just sat and cried together. Despite the heartache she and her girls had been through and the loss she still felt, Aunt Sal told me, "Collin's death is the worst thing that has ever happened to our family."

Almost seven years after Uncle Bob's death, Dad's sister Peg's husband was killed in a car crash on the way home after his shift as a Delaware State Trooper. They had four boys under the age of eight. Aunt Peg and I talked about how to manage our reeling emotions while rearing our children and how to help them deal with their own grief. We lamented the way some friends drift away because they don't know how to deal with those who grieve. Aunt Peg reminisced about Collin and hugged me as I cried. She said a cardinal visited her yard every day and that when he chirped, her young grandson Zachary said, "Nana, there's Collin again!"

English writer and critic Samuel Johnson wrote, "Where grief is fresh, any attempt to divert it only irritates." My aunts knew just what I needed. They never pushed me to "get over" my grief and provided me a safe place to vent and sob and question and remember. They were there for me "when the stillness [came]."[15]

Most of my friends were supportive too, although few had the patience to listen to the same unanswerable existential questions for the thousandth time or the experience to deal with despair. I know they all would have done anything I asked. The problem was, I

---

[15] Columnist Charles M. Blow wrote that after his brother's funeral, a relative consoled him by saying, "We'll be here when the stillness comes." Charles M. Blow, "My Brother Died and Reminded Me of These Life Lessons," *New York Times* (Oct. 14, 2020), Retrieved from https://www.nytimes.com/2020/10/14/opinion/brother-death-lessons.html?referringSource=articleShare.

couldn't ask. Trapped in my cocoon, I couldn't reach out. They say times like these show you who your true friends are, and some of the results were surprising.

I didn't hear from my best friend for six months. (Recently, I learned that she was dealing with her own traumas.) My school buddy called frequently but pressed so hard for me to see a psychiatrist that I stopped answering her calls. Other friends just drifted away. But Meg, whom I hadn't seen in a while, called regularly. She was caring yet kept the conversation lively and upbeat. Betty, the mother of three of my students, called and visited weekly with armfuls of flowers from her garden. My next-door neighbor Ellen invited me to go to line-dancing classes with her. Joanne, my former next-door neighbor, and Gail, my friend since kindergarten, called regularly and really listened. Gail, who was studying to be a chaplain, set a powerful example of faith without preaching or pushing me to turn to God. When I apologized for never being the one to call, she told me she'd let me know when it was my turn. It's still not my turn.

I also had to leave the house to meet with mental health providers. Before paying out any funds, my disability insurance company required proof that I was unable to work. I had to meet with two different psychiatrists and convince them I was incapacitated even though I was lucid and looked normal. I understand that this keeps people from gaming the system, but it was distressing to be in such pain and barely be able to take care of myself yet have to explain why I lacked the emotional stamina, creativity, and motivation to teach children all day.

Once my disability was approved, I had to meet regularly with a psychiatrist who would periodically recertify my depression (grief was not a recognized psychiatric disorder). Finding a provider was a nightmare. People who need mental health services are at their lowest point, sometimes unable to get out of bed, make a phone call, or even focus. You'd think there would be a system or service to help us obtain care. Nope. I was on my own. Unbeknownst to me, my health insurer had a reputation of not paying providers, so most doctors refused to deal with it. I called more than thirty psychiatrists before I found one who would see me. Just making the calls was traumatic, as the phone was a stressor for me. Sometimes it took me several days to get up the nerve to dial.

Navigating the mental health care system wasn't like the movies, in which the psychiatrist is empathetic and caring, says all the right things, and prescribes just the right medicine cocktail to make you feel better. Instead, it was like wandering in the wilderness, desperately searching for help. These guys added to my stress.

When I visited my first psychiatrist, the receptionist had to unlock the door to let me into the waiting area. *A bad sign,* I thought. *Is he afraid of his patients?* The doctor seemed distracted and sometimes ate popcorn during our session (no, he never offered me any). One day I showed up for an appointment and no one was there. The receptionist had left a message on my answering machine at home, but I had come directly from school. The office had that phone number on all the forms I had filled out. Later, they tried to charge me for an appointment I did not miss. Petty stuff, I know, until you're depressed and everything is an effort.

My next psychiatrist was worse. On a good day, he was gruff like Dennis the Menace's neighbor Mr. Wilson—but with no hint of any soft heart beneath the bluster. He implied that my problems were trivial compared to those of his alcoholic and drug-addicted patients and scolded me for arriving late for an appointment. Really? I was doing the best I could. Depression and grief can make it hard to complete the tasks necessary to get out the door. That day, they got the better of me. He also refused to complete anyone's disability insurance certifications but neglected to warn me until I handed him one. This forced me to ask my primary care physician. He resisted at first because Mean Mr. Wilson told him I needed to go back to work, although he had never suggested that to me.

Third time's the charm? No. The next psychiatrist seemed nice enough, until he wasn't. Even though he scheduled appointments, most patients waited an hour or two before being seen. One day he complained that I was asking questions about things he had already gone over. I had trouble understanding his pronounced accent, and sometimes it took me a minute to process what he said. By then, I had a question, but he had moved on to another point. After we finished our session, I realized I had forgotten to ask him to sign my insurance certification and had to go back into his office. The doctor berated me until I finally said, "Stop yelling at me!" "I'm not yelling," he yelled. I burst into tears. "You're not trying to get better," he said. Read: none of the medications he prescribed was working, so it was my fault. He gave me a box of tissues and let me calm down. When I checked out at the receptionist's counter, he brought a peace offering—a mug and pen, freebies from some drug rep.

So maybe psychiatrists are focused on prescribing meds and don't expend a lot of energy on bedside manner, right? A therapist would certainly be more empathetic. But my first counselor spent more time telling me how stoically she coped with her parents' deaths than listening to me. She seemed to believe everyone experienced loss the same way and should handle it as she so competently had. But as Shakespeare wrote, "Well, every one can master a grief but he that has it." This woman hadn't buried her child. She regaled me with stories of her clients who had "made lemonade" out of loss and found new meaning after their loved ones' deaths by throwing themselves into volunteer work or starting charitable foundations. "That's life. There's nothing you can do. Just get over it," she said (yes, she actually said that). My son had been gone just six weeks and I could barely take a shower, but she wanted me to start a foundation. Afterward, I sat in the car and sobbed.

Finally my insurance changed and so did my fortunes. My next therapist, Barbara, probably coached movie doctors. She was wonderful, and I left her office each week feeling positive and hopeful. We worked together (this was an actual collaboration) for several years until she said she didn't think I needed her anymore.

A few months later, my new psychiatrist required that I also see one of her practice's therapists. For the next decade, these two women provided amazing care that turned into friendship. I had finally found the people who would guide and support me through my depression and grief.

Dr. C. was personable and engaged, and she asked for and remembered details about my family and noticed if I changed my hairstyle. She knew how each medication acted and told me how other patients had responded to them. She continually tweaked my medications to find the right combination.

Talking to my therapist never felt like therapy. It was more like chatting with a friend, without the fear that she was just being polite or would get sick of hearing my problems over and over. Beth listened to me and told personal stories to illuminate my concerns and give me perspective. Unlike my first counselor, she never implied that I needed to do things a certain way. Rather than constantly asking the aggravating "And how did that make you feel?" she deftly channeled the conversation into a discussion of the underlying issues.

Unfortunately, my association with both ended recently. A widow, Dr. C. remarried and moved to be with her new husband in New York. And when I turned sixty-five, Beth told me that Medicare didn't recognize her certification. My new psychiatrist seems competent but lacks Dr. C.'s rapport. So far she hasn't insisted I find another counselor.

It saddens me to think of how many other people struggle to find capable mental health support. Every profession has some less-than-stellar practitioners, but being subjected to incompetence, insensitivity, and cruelty is an especially egregious blow to an individual at her lowest point, just trying to survive each day. A helper who not only doesn't help, but makes things worse, is demoralizing and potentially dangerous. I finally found excellent providers, but it shouldn't have taken a decade.

Twenty-first Century Porn

Why do we grieve, "if not in hope of beauty laid bare, life heightened and its deepest mystery probed?" Author Annie Dillard wrote those words to explain why we write, but they serve just as well as a goal for grief work. Isn't our ultimate intent to memorialize our beloved, live a meaningful life, and discern the mysteries of life and death and God?

If grief is charged with this higher mandate, why do people treat it as indulgent self-pity? Take a Prozac and go back to work in the morning. How did our mourning rituals desiccate into nuisances? Why does sorrow make people uncomfortable? When did death become, as anthropologist Geoffrey Gorer asked, "the new pornography"?[16]

Grief is a toe in the water of the universe. Can we afford to pass enlightenment on the freeway in our Lexuses and Suburbans as we smugly multitask breakfast, makeup, and barks into the cell phone? What if the answers we seek are there in the relationships we have subrogated into e-mail jokes and the soccer carpool? Sociologist Emile Durkheim said, "[A] family [community] which allows one of its members to die without being wept for shows by that very fact that it lacks moral unity and cohesion . . .; it renounces its existence." Shouldn't we support and encourage those who, as our proxies,

---

[16] Geoffrey Gorer, Death, Grief and Mourning.

accept the pain of the search? Perhaps the wet-toed must insist that grief be obliged, since the untested are as oblivious to its virtue as a child is to the value of eating peas.

TLC

A Buddhist maxim notes, "When you are born, you cry, and the world rejoices. When you die, you rejoice, and the world cries." Newborn Collin was celebrated; teen Collin was certainly wept for.

Many people also told us they prayed for Collin, and hundreds participated in the coast-to-coast prayer vigil Aunt Sal organized that Friday night in the hospital. Others, like my friend Gail, told us they added Collin and our family to their prayer chains or church "Joys and Concerns" lists. Many continued to ask for prayers and comfort for us after Collin died. Our Catholic friends sent mass cards to let us know that prayers would be said in Collin's memory.

I had never had much use for prayer. I had never been taught to talk to God, only to recite the Our Father, Hail Mary, and Apostles' Creed I'd had to memorize as a child in CCD. Our family attended mass and received the sacraments, and my father raced through grace each night before dinner, but my family had never done bedtime prayers or even discussed prayer. I was ambivalent about God, uncertain whether he—or she—interfered in human lives even if he or she existed. It should be enough to live by the golden rule and be kind and generous, I thought. When Collin lay in the hospital and I was desperate to believe anything that might save him, I tried to remember those childhood prayers. Unsuccessful, I spoke directly to God, although it pretty much devolved into me taunting him. I felt sheepish even asking—that friend who only calls when she needs something—when I'd never had a relationship with God before.

Although they didn't keep Collin alive, I was surprised to find everyone's prayers extremely comforting. Just knowing that people were thinking of us, cared about us, meant so much. Later I would read several books on the power of prayer and intention to change outcomes, but it was my loved ones' prayers for my family that changed my views on its value.

Even before the funeral, the flowers started arriving. Vases and baskets of gorgeous roses, carnations, Gerber daisies, iris, and mixed flowers brightened our mourning and teased out smiles. The fragrances filled our home and triggered memories of prom corsages, the red roses (one more every year) my dad gave my mom for their anniversary, the bouquets Ed sent me just because, and the tiny nosegays Collin picked for me. They recalled the prize Tropicana rose bush, peonies, and tulips Irénée du Pont had gifted my grandfather, his painter, from the Granogue estate garden. As a toddler I plucked the tulips at the bud and presented them to my grandmother. Peace lilies, stargazer lilies, and my favorite calla lilies symbolized peace and hope and the transcendence of Collin's soul. Daffodil bouquets from my friend Betty reminded us that life endures, reborn after a cold, dark winter.

Some people sent plants, rather than cut flowers. These were in large pots or baskets or dish gardens, all lush green, some with floral accents. Lasting months, rather than days, they exuded calm and energizing oxygen to replace what was constantly being sucked out of the room. The care they required kept us all alive.

And then there were the sympathy and "thinking of you" cards and personal notes, more than four hundred in all. Cards came from our friends, family, neighbors; our coworkers, Ed's clients, and my students' families; our parents', siblings', and children's friends; Collin's classmates, his fellow radio broadcasting students, his baseball team, his chemistry class, his teachers, the people he worked with at Best Buy. People sent cards while Collin was in the hospital, then again after he died.

Some people sent several. My mother's friend Ginny sent a card every month for a year. Kelly sent cards and notes every few days, sharing her own grief and Collin memories. I could drag myself to the mailbox if I thought there might be cards waiting. Opening each envelope enveloped us in a warm hug, and the beautiful images of flowers, stars, butterflies, birds, angels, and sunsets carried symbolism of rebirth, metamorphosis, timelessness, and a connection to the divine.

The cards' poetic messages soothed my writer's soul. I envisioned each sender browsing at Hallmark, then deciding, *Yes, the sentiment on this card is the perfect one for the Robinsons.* My favorite was inspired by an Eskimo legend: "Perhaps they are not the stars, but rather openings in Heaven where the love of our lost ones pours through and shines down upon us to let us know they are happy." Another was from the final pages of Antoine de Saint-Exupéry's *The Little Prince:* "In one of the stars I shall be living. In one of them I shall be laughing. And so it will be as if all the stars were laughing, when you look at the sky at night." Perhaps I was drawn to such messages since we had adopted stars as our symbol for Collin. It comforted me to think of him as still laughing and happy, watching over and loving us from the heavens.

Even more heartening than the cards themselves were the personal messages people added. Love poured from every word as they expressed their own shock and grief and sought to help shoulder ours. My sister wrote, "I miss him terribly. I can only imagine how you are feeling, as I am sure my loss . . . cannot be half as great as the loss you are feeling, missing Collin every day that he does not come home." The mother of Collin's friend Dominick summed up the sentiments of so many: "I can't imagine the devastation this has taken on your family but I pray that each day may be a little easier to bear without Collin."

Others shared memories of the boy they knew. "He was so special, and such a joy!" wrote Collin's kindergarten teacher. She had worked closely with us as we struggled to get a diagnosis for his tics and behavior. At the time, she assured us that he was not a problem in school, just "all boy!" Collin's third grade teacher remembered him as "a freckled-face, nature-loving little boy. . . . Collin was not the kind of child to be forgotten. He touched all of us." Her teammate, Lee, had also taught Collin. In true Delaware one-degree-of-separation fashion, Lee later became my colleague and friend. She sent several notes. Shortly after Christmas, she wrote, "Collin was the light that filled your family with hope . . . or, perhaps, the angel that poised itself on the top of your tree, smiling peacefully upon you." Lee also let me know I was missed: "No one could replace your knowledge, your creativity, or your high expectations for all children. No one notices until you are not here."

This was gratifying, as even though I felt too emotionally broken to return to teaching, I missed the fun of my students parading in their handmade Greek tunics and piling books onto toothpick bridges to test their strength, the thrill of Nick creating an edible drinking straw for our Invention Convention, and seeing exhilaration spread across Jaleesa's face as she finished her first drawing on the computer. Helping children "become" was part of my DNA, and I mourned this loss along with my son.

Cards and notes from my students and their parents helped. Mary wrote, "Cody, Charlie and I miss you at Highlands." She thanked us for the "beautiful pictures from baby to teenager" displayed at the viewing, as they "gave a glimpse of [Collin's] personality and the love in your family." A few families sent books on grief or inspirational music tapes. I even got a card and note from Lisa, a third-grader in my first class twenty years before.

My friend Francine, our school's art teacher, brought me a box of cards my students had made. At the time, I taught several groups of talented and gifted (TAG) students, as well as computer skills to all classes. One teacher had stuck a Post-it on her class's cards: "Francine, These will rip your heart out!" Indeed, the cards were precious, and I cried over every one. The covers featured colorful hearts, flowers, angels, and computers, with the tiniest details such as a stack of books individually titled *Sorry / Mrs. Robinson / Colon* [sic] */ Sympathy*; little pop-up hearts and stars; angels crying; and "a chair for you to sit in whenever your [sic] sad." One card was a thumbnail-sized booklet.

Inside, most sentiments were variations on this one (spelling errors and all!): "Dear Mrs. Robinson, I'm very very sorry about what happened to Colin. It's not the same when your not teaching computers. Our whole class really misses you. your cool, Lizzy."

Andrew wrote, "I hope your son will be you guardian angle!" Nicolai's card said he was sorry and missed me. He added, "I made a book about the Fibonacci[17] in tag (to get extra credit)." He knew I'd appreciate that. I chuckled at Amanda's note: "The substitute is nice but if there was an emmy for computer teacher's, I bet you would win twice."

Heartfelt messages also came from people I barely knew. Bereaved mothers offered condolences from heartbroken experience and added their phone numbers, knowing I would need to talk. Their notes reminded me that we are not solitary entities, but supported by others in our community through a vast web of interconnections, many of which we may not even be aware.

I am part of a large, loving family, and Mom's work as a substitute teacher and church choir director and Dad's work as a teacher, principal, superintendent, and NEA director created multiple circles of friends. We often joked that Dad knew everyone in Delaware and couldn't even travel overseas without meeting someone he knew. My parents' childhood friends, neighbors and former neighbors, former and current colleagues, bridge groups, the "Saturday night" group, and the church friends watched me grow up, marry, and have children. They knew our stories and became a second family, proud of our accomplishments and ready to help when we needed it. And of course, Ed and I and our kids had our own friends. But until Collin died, I had no idea how far all these connections stretched or how many there were.

"Our kids play ball at Swift [Park], go to the same schools," wrote the mother of Collin's classmate Kate. "We live in the same community. Ed and his help have beautified our home. Though we're not friends, we share much. . . . We're sorry for your tremendous loss."

The St. Marks's choir and orchestra performed their Easter cantata the day before Collin died. Mom and Katie debated whether to

---

[17] The Fibonacci sequence is a sequence of numbers in which each number is the sum of the previous two: 1, 1, 2, 3, 5, 8 . . . . The mathematical explanation for the "golden ratio," it explains spiral-like natural patterns such as the arrangement of sunflower seeds and manmade ones such as the behavior of financial markets. Although known in India since the 6th century, it was popularized in early 11th century Europe by Leonardo Bonacci, a mathematician from Pisa later known as Fibonacci.

participate but decided to go ahead after the doctors said Collin would probably stabilize over the next week. A choir member sent heartfelt condolences and added that she and her husband "enjoyed to the fullest the wonderful contribution to the program of music the Glynn and Robinson families have made. My heart went out to Kathleen on Sunday when I saw her at her 'post' playing the flute!"

We also didn't know Collin had volunteered as a student aide until his chemistry teacher wrote that he often explained difficult concepts to other students and added, "He was *extremely* helpful in grading work and in doing some word processing for me."

I pored over every card and letter and read each again and again. I still have them all today. These were small acts of compassion, but their collective impact was—is—massive. Such condolences are the glue that binds families and communities and guarantees that "You'll Never Walk Alone." Just as "our people" sustained us during five days in the hospital, their presence, loving gestures, and words got us through another agonizing five days as we waited to say goodbye to our Collin. Throughout the past decades, they shone bright moments into dark days, reminded me that I wasn't alone, and kept Collin's memory alive.

They probably helped keep me alive as well. Words have power—the power to change history, to excite ideas, to move mountains. But they have no power over death. They cannot do the one thing I want more than anything else—bring Collin back.

Honor Roll

*A*fter the funeral, people continued to call and send cards, notes, mass cards, flowers, and meals. Others donated in Collin's name to the Tourette Syndrome Association.[18] Still others sent gifts of stars, angel figurines, wall plaques, picture frames, or books. These are vivid remembrances of Collin.

Several people wrote poems to honor him. Collin's cousin Art's poem included the lines, "The skies will never be as blue . . . As the one whose spirit will shine brightly forever, As the one whose soul reaches deep within our cavernous hearts, As the one we all know as Collin." Aunt Peg wrote an acrostic, in which each letter in COLLIN / ANGEL / STAR began a word that described him: Courteous, Optimistic, Leader. . . . Chuck, Collin's friend, wrote, "But the deed is done / The white feathered angel is weeping / Came and took, the brother, son, and friend."

Others tapped their creative reservoirs, as well. Aunt Sal created a video slideshow of Collin photos accompanied by music. My cousin Beth made a mix tape. Kelly had a star in the constellation Perseus[19] named in his memory. My mom's friend Sandy cross-stitched copies of my thank-you notes with the *Romeo and Juliet* quotation, paint swash, and stars. She gave one to us and one to my parents. For five

---

[18] Now the Tourette Association of America.
[19] Perseus was the Greek hero who slew Medusa and rescued Andromeda from the sea monster.

years, my friend Meg and her daughter, Amanda, made Christmas ornaments with Collin's name on them. We put some on our home tree and others on Collin's tree at the cemetery. Sarah, Collin's classmate, sent us a dogwood tree.

Other unselfish gestures showed how much people cared. Someone made a large anonymous donation to help cover funeral expenses. Our friends Doreen, the church organist, and Bert, the soloist, refused payment for their services, instead donating the money to the church music fund. My friend and neighbor Joyce answered Ed's business calls and arranged for neighbors to bring us dinners. My friend and neighbor Antoinette, the mother of Katie's friend Stefania and Collin's friends Giancarlo and Franco, shared dreams about Collin. She has put a blanket of greens on his grave every Christmas. Mike, Matt's former guidance counselor, stopped by to see how he was doing.

The year he died, Collin's school yearbook featured a page with his photo and a note of memoriam. We funded a scholarship at the school. In a nod to Collin's radio and computer interests, it was awarded to a student who showed achievement in one of those areas. The first winner was Barbara, a foreign exchange student from Germany who also dreamed of a career as a radio announcer. In her thank-you note, she shared a memory of Collin:

> My impression of Collin changed rapidly throughout the year. At the beginning I thought of him as a quiet person but after I got to know him better, I met the funny Collin who was always joking around. Every time he was willing to help us out, especially if there were any problems on the computer.

Collin's radio broadcasting teacher (who was also the baseball coach who gave him the wrong size uniform on that awful day) created a large bulletin board in his classroom that noted Collin's achievements and character and included photos plus comments and memories from his fellow students. The display was a lovely accolade, but my heart sank to see Collin's name misspelled as "Colin."

Collin's class planted a kousa dogwood tree in his memory and installed a plaque with his name beneath it. Unfortunately, again, his name was spelled "Colin." I couldn't understand how his teacher and

112

his school could get his name wrong. I'm a teacher, and I can't conceive of misspelling a student's name. Although their intentions were honorable, it still cut to the bone. When someone dies, all that is left are memories, photographs, and his or her name. Such a small detail, yet such an enormous impact.

A family friend took it upon himself to set things right. Tripp had coached Matt's baseball team, and his father was the school principal. Our kids had all gone to school together. Tripp was a scout for the San Diego Padres and arranged for the baseball team to sponsor a replacement plaque with Collin's name spelled correctly. Collin would have thought this was cool.

Collin's friend Peter asked to borrow our old Apple IIGS computer so he could play *The Black Cauldron* and the other video games he and Collin had spent hours on when computers were new. And one day he, Jonathan, and Giancarlo asked to hang out in Collin's room. We invited each to choose something of Collin's as a memento.

I collected "Collin" songs—lyrics that reminded me of him. After I bought Sarah McLachlan's *Surfacing*, I listened to it three times from start to finish and then put "Angel" on replay. My other favorite album is *Somewhere Between Heaven and Earth*, which Cindy Bullens wrote after her eleven-year-old daughter Jessie died from cancer. Each track reflects a different aspect of grief, and it's as if Bullens mined my emotions. "Why," by Rascal Flatts, is about someone who died by suicide, but its powerful message of missing someone gone too soon is matched only by its plaintive melody. Queen's "Who Wants to Live Forever" provided the musical backdrop to a scene in the film *Highlander* in which the main character's wife dies. Freddie Mercury's rendition of Brian May's lyrics haunts me. Green Day's Billie Joe Armstrong wrote "Wake Me Up When September Comes" for his father who died when Billie Joe was a child. When I listen, I substitute April for September. And John Fogerty's "Centerfield" lets me remember happier times—six-year-old Collin oblivious to a ball hit past him in the outfield because he was busy playing with the ants.

At first I swapped actual CDs in and out of the player. Then iTunes came out and I made a playlist on my computer. Eventually the songs made it to my iPod and finally, my iPhone. My list stands currently at eighty-six songs. I still listen when I'm melancholy or need a connection with Collin.

In a corner of our family room, we created a memory space for Collin. We hung a copy of Kelly's eulogy with Collin's photo, the star certificate, the cross-stitched *Romeo and Juliet* quotation, a plaque that reads "Never give up," and a string banner of stars and feathers. Later we added a line from one of my poems on a plaque, a Christmas present from Kelly. On a corner shelf, we placed the poems people had written, our favorite sympathy cards, a ceramic figurine of a little boy in a blue swimsuit who looked like Collin, a Beanie Baby angel holding a star, and an Orioles' Cal Ripken bobblehead. I can't pass the space without looking at the items, much like a Jewish mother touching a *mezuzah* every time she enters her home.

Eight years after Collin died, we converted his room into a nursery for his new cousin, Maggie. Butterflies flutter where his sharks swam, and his now-pastel toy trunk is filled with baby blankets. He would have loved the high ledge that now circles the room as a great place to display his rocks. Dismantling Collin's room was heart-wrenching, but it felt like we had been giving him away piece by piece for months, as we unpinned his Best Buy nametag from his work shirt, threw out his toothbrush and battered Nikes . . . bagged his clothes and handed them to the man with no teeth at Goodwill . . . tucked away his class ring and traded in his car . . . buried Sparckey . . .

We couldn't bear to throw away all the things that reminded us of Collin. So on the anniversary of his death that year, our extended family got together and decorated a smaller room with his photos, cat figurines, baseball memorabilia, *South Park* cartoons, stars, and video game trappings. We stenciled tone-on-tone stars on one wall, and Kelly made curtains to match a star mirror. We put up shelves, hung photos, created shadowboxes, and filled a corner cupboard.

Of course, the best memorial is the one Collin initiated himself. His gifts of life alleviated much suffering and allowed desperately sick people to live normal lives again.

Collin's heart gave new life to Tony, who is married with three sons, allowing him to return to work full-time as a salesman. Tony sent us a long letter and apologized for not writing sooner. Before the transplant, he had been in the hospital for three-and-a-half months. "I found it very difficult to accept that for me to continue my life someone would have to give up theirs," he wrote. He said he and his family thank us every day.

Six-year-old Ahmad was freed from the restrictions of dialysis when he received one of Collin's kidneys. His parents and siblings each signed the letter to us that began, "With reverence do we write this letter to you. . . . We will never even find words to express all that we want to say or explain our innermost feelings and thoughts to you." They offered sincere condolences and hoped that we might find hope and peace in knowing that Collin's loss gave someone else new life.

The recipient of Collin's other kidney and his liver was a thirty-nine-year-old married man who had been unable to work because of his illness. Two people can see again through Collin's kind eyes. Cells that produced insulin in his pancreas were transplanted into patients with diabetes, and although Collin's lungs were unsuitable for transplant because he contracted pneumonia while on the ventilator, they were used for research.

The combination of a not-fully-developed teenaged prefrontal cortex and Tourette Syndrome impulsivity allowed the emotional behavior that led to Collin's accident. But his final, unselfish act was the mature, responsible decision of an adult.

V
Playing Pecos Bill

This grief has a life
unto itself beyond
my control; challenging
me, taunting,
sucking up even the oxygen
as it passes; carrying me
along as it twists and spins, spitting
out bits of me at every turn; daring
me to play Pecos Bill.

Firsts Strike

When you have a baby, the first year is filled with exciting events—her first smile, her first experience eating solid food, his first tooth, his first steps. There are trips to Grandma's, the zoo, and the beach. Every holiday is bathed in new light as you honor family rituals and create new ones.

When your child dies, the firsts are heartbreaking. The first Mother's and Father's Days without him. The first Christmas with no presents under the tree tagged with her name. The first birthday with no cake. The first visit to someone in the hospital where your beloved died. Even if you've managed to maneuver through most days without a breakdown, each first strikes with the grief monster's full wrath, and it ravages your emotions like Godzilla tearing through Tokyo. Your child dies all over again.

Mother's Day was just six weeks after Collin died. At the cemetery and later at home, I cried bittersweet tears, remembering Collin's birth. On Mother's Day in 1981, I had mild contractions off and on all day. We enjoyed the warm sun and chatted with our next-door neighbors Dave and Joanne while their son, Jarett, and Matt rode their Big Wheels. The next morning my labor progressed and we went to the hospital. Collin was born that afternoon. Hard labor was short and the birth easy. I always thought of Collin as my Mother's Day gift.

I was grateful to spend this Mother's Day with Matt and Katie, and Ed's and my parents came over for dinner, which helped. But competing emotions jousted for my attention, happiness and misery creating a cognitive dissonance. Although I tried to enjoy the attention from my children and celebrate my mother and mother-in-law, a neon sign in my mind flashed and throbbed like a migraine—Collin is missing.

Just as it had in 1981, May 11, 1998, fell on a Monday, so Collin's seventeenth birthday was again the day after Mother's Day. Ed and I took flowers to his grave, a place simultaneously comforting and agonizing. I felt close to him there, as I did in his room, but hated that I had to come to such a place, with my son trapped underground in a concrete tomb. Again I replayed his birth, but tried to focus on the joy it brought us. Still, I railed at the cruel force that stomped on his future. Until the tragedy, Collin's sixteenth year had been his best ever, as he learned to drive, got a job at Best Buy, made new friends, and began to be noticed by girls. The next should have been even better. As on Mother's Day, the day improved when our parents joined us for a dinner of Collin's favorites—ravioli, mozzarella sticks, and his famous apple pizza. Stubborn, I even baked Aunt Sally's chocolate cake and we sang "Happy Birthday," although we bypassed the candles.

Although not as difficult as Collin's birthday, other family birthdays that first year brought their own challenges. Dad's birthday was just a week after we buried Collin. Life stops for nothing, not even death, and like waves breaking on the beach it relentlessly pounded us with demands that we show up, participate, interact, and be grateful for what—and who—remained. We came together for dinner, and my Mom made her Million-Dollar Pound Cake, but the mood was more somber than festive.

My brother's birthday came five days after Collin's and Kelly's two weeks after that. Jeff lived in Annapolis and Kelly in Fort Lauderdale, so there were no expectations for parties. Kelly, who had been so close to Collin, struggled with feeling sad while being so far away, and she and I had a long, tearful phone conversation.

The next birthday was my forty-fourth. I was probably at the midpoint of my life, I realized. Although there had certainly been challenges, such as dealing with Collin's TS, the first half had been pretty charmed. I had grown up with loving parents and a supportive extended family, done well in school, married my high school sweetheart, become a successful teacher, bought a house, and

120

had three happy kids and good friends. I set and achieved goals, enjoyed new adventures, and looked eagerly to the future. But it was as if I had been shoved through an enchanted mirror and couldn't find a way back out. Was this karma? Did I have to "pay" for those good years? Would the second half of my life—trapped on the dark side of the mirror—be as awful as the first half had been good? Is grief, as Queen Elizabeth II said, "the price we pay for love"?

Ed's dad's birthday was in July. We surely got together for dinner, but I have no specific memories of the day. The same is true of both our mothers' birthdays, which are lost in the blur of fall, from back-to-school through the knockout punch of the holidays. Ed's and Katie's birthdays came on the same day in August. Katie turned thirteen, and I tried to make a big deal about her becoming a teenager. Ed just endured his day the way I had mine, probably with his own questions.

The last first birthday after Collin's death was Matt's twentieth, in January 1999. He had flunked out of college and was working with Ed. He spent his free time sequestered in his room with friends. I fretted that, consumed by my own grief, I had not cushioned his. Every morning I breathed a sigh of relief when I heard him thump up the stairs.

The hits just kept coming. Father's Day was *Groundhog Day,*[20] a replay of Mother's Day. Ed's anguish magnified my own. It felt wrong to have only two of our three children with us, and we all dodged the gaping hole in the room and hid the ones in our hearts. It was as poet Edna St. Vincent Millay noted: "Where you used to be, there is a hole in the world, which I find myself constantly walking around in the daytime, and falling in at night. I miss you like hell."

The holidays were always a whirlwind of excitement and activity. From Halloween through New Year's, there were celebrations to plan, parties to attend, food to cook, rituals to observe, and new traditions to create. Without Collin, some of that simply stopped. Other things continued, with tears amid the smiles. And some events were just too painful to bear. My depression worsened, if that were possible, and I

---

[20] A film starring Bill Murray, in which his character woke up every morning and relived the day before.

slogged in cement shoes through days that gathered speed like a locomotive steaming downhill with no brakes. I tried to keep things as normal as possible for Matt and Katie while devising new customs that honored Collin.

Halloween was one of Collin's favorite holidays. Our candy boy loved trick-or-treating, stuffing a bag with goodies. He never put much effort into his costume—a hideous rubber mask was good enough—but he was entranced by the *idea* of the holiday. One year he convinced me that we should build a haunted house in our garage. We used boxes to set up the walls of a maze, and at each turn you'd confront a dangling spider, a moaning ghost, bowls of eyeballs and intestines, a glow-in-the-dark skeleton, or Dracula rising from his coffin. The designing and creating was as much fun as the final walk-through.

Princess and T-Rex costumes aside, it's hard now to think about Halloween without its associated theme of death. After Collin died, the holiday became truly macabre. Remembering our fake Dracula coffin conjured images of Collin in his real one, wearing khakis and a blue Henley shirt instead of a tuxedo. Styrofoam tombstones stuck in front lawns reminded us that Collin had his own, honest-to-goodness granite tombstone with his name chiseled into it. The holiday's signature colors popped up everywhere, dredging up our horror at Collin's original orange and black memorial. I cringed when children danced on our front porch dressed as skeletons or ghosts. Even Jack-o-lanterns mocked our grief. "Lighten up! Have fun!" they leered.

I had barely processed Halloween and it was time for Thanksgiving. Thanksgiving. Sure. None of us was in a thankful mood. Of course we were grateful for one another, for our home, for good food—but grief has a way of trumping joy. The conversation, usually lively, was muted. No one knew what to say. Even the yelling at the football teams on TV was halfhearted. We left a chair empty at the table and toasted Collin, and I thought how incongruous it was to be raising a glass to him at sixteen, instead of celebrating him and a bride. My mother's turkey dinner was spectacular, as always, but all I could think about was the year of the Thanksgiving nachos.

Collin was eight or nine, and his TS had been especially onerous, with him arguing and raging at everything. The week leading up to the holiday had been exhausting, and my nerves were so frayed that I canceled our trip to my brother's home in Virginia. I couldn't bring myself to smile and pretend everything was fine. My parents rescued us, whisking the kids to Virginia to gorge on my sister-in-law Marybeth's gourmet turkey and fixins while Ed and I tore into the Tostitos in front of the TV.

Whether you're ready or not, Christmas starts the day after Thanksgiving. Gifts to buy, a house and tree to decorate, cookies to bake, special events and parties to attend. . . . Even the thought overwhelmed me. Ed and I debated whether to ignore Christmas or go away somewhere the year Collin died. But we didn't want to be away from our extended family just when we needed one another's support. Plus, Matt and Katie had endured multiple changes to their routines, and it seemed cruel to deprive them of a bit of happiness. I didn't want things to devolve to "Collin died, and that's why we can't do fun things." Honoring some of our holiday traditions would reassure them that they were important too and that what they cared about mattered.

We talked with the kids about which traditions to keep and which would go on hiatus. Our calendar breathed a sigh of relief as we decided to forego the parties, events, and visits that usually filled every weekend in December. We did, however, go to my parents' for Christmas Eve dinner and visited both sets of parents on Christmas Day. We bought gifts for our kids and other loved ones. I did not decorate the house, a task that normally took an entire weekend, except to put out Collin's nutcracker collection.

Everyone was excited to decorate a tree for Collin's grave. We bought a three-foot potted Alberta spruce and dressed it with garlands and lights (the batteries burned out the first night). Everyone brought weather-friendly ornaments, and my friend Meg and her daughter contributed shiny blue orbs on which they had written Collin's name in glitter. Collin's friend Giancarlo's mother covered the grave with a blanket of greens, and my parents staked down a soldier nutcracker to keep watch.

We considered not getting a tree for our home, but in the end, decided to decorate a Fraser fir with only stars, our symbol for Collin. We invited friends and family to contribute stars and bought some ourselves. The result was magical. Everyone thinks their Christmas tree is beautiful, but "Collin's tree" was magnificent. There were stars of silver, gold, brass, glass, crystal, plastic, wood, beads, shells, paper, ribbons, cast iron, ceramic, fabric, lace, and yarn. Some were flat and others three-dimensional. Starbursts of all different sizes included five-, six-, and eight-pointed stars, Moravian stars, and Stars of Bethlehem.

Some were so large we had to prop them up lest they weigh down the branches and others so small and delicate I later had to make sure they didn't get thrown away with the tree. Each star glittered and shone, and even though the tree lights were white, many of the ornaments reflected prismatic colors. The perfect conical evergreen seemed lit from within, enveloped in a warm aura that exuded love and comfort. We told ourselves Collin had coordinated the awe-inspiring effect. Although we've tried to replicate it each year since, none has come close to matching the enchantment of that first star tree.

Even with no entertainment events, December was arduous. I could only bear to shop for presents about one day a week, as I was besieged by gifts I might have purchased for Collin—Henley shirts, khakis, Timberland boots, baseball bats and gloves, baseball cards, Toblerone chocolate.... He would have loved *Half-Life,* the alien invasion scenario video game. Mentally, I stayed tense, prepared for whatever might pop up around the next corner, so I wouldn't end up blubbering in the aisle.

Christmas carols singing of new birth and joy were daggers in my heart. Although I had always pulled out the holiday music the day after Thanksgiving, I didn't cue up the Philadelphia Orchestra's *The Joy of Christmas* or Ray Conniff's *We Wish You a Merry Christmas* for years. I felt like an imposter among the other shoppers, their faces bright as they enjoyed the sights and sounds of the thrill of the search while I tried to finish my chore as quickly as possible, hunched over so I wouldn't run into anyone I knew.

After an hour or two, I fled to my car. Eight months, and life still incapacitated me. There was no joy in Robinsonville.[21] At home, I curled up in my dark closet and cried. I needed that sanctuary, needed not to talk to anyone, needed to erase the images of shiny Christmas balls, twinkling lights, gaudy packages, bright carols,

---

[21] A play on "There is no joy in Whoville," from *How the Grinch Stole Christmas* by Dr. Seuss.

124

smiles and laughter. At other times I wanted to be near and see my family but wished I could be an invisible presence like a spirit in Charles Dickens' *A Christmas Carol*—the Ghost of Christmas Past. C. S. Lewis's description of grief was my perfect costume:

> No one ever told me that grief felt so like fear. I am not afraid, but the sensation is like being afraid. The same fluttering in the stomach, the same restlessness, the yawning. I keep on swallowing. . . . At other times it feels like being mildly drunk, or concussed. There is a sort of invisible blanket between the world and me. I find it hard to take in what anyone says. Or perhaps, hard to want to take it in. It is so uninteresting. Yet I want the others to be about me. I dread the moments when the house is empty. If only they would talk to one another and not to me.

All kids love getting Christmas presents, but Collin loved giving them. He chose each carefully and watched eagerly as they were opened. Since he would not be thumping down the stairs on Christmas morning, his arms piled high with gifts for us, we asked our loved ones to send some instead—stories and memories about Collin. As these arrived, we placed them in Collin's stocking. While we shared brunch with our extended family, we opened each story gift and read it aloud.

We had heard some of the tales before, like the time Grammy and Grandfather took new driver Collin to scope out the University of Tennessee. They let him drive the last leg, and he took the off-ramp into Knoxville at sixty miles per hour despite Grandfather stomping on his imaginary passenger seat brake. Others were new, like the time Collin and Giancarlo wanted to go to a movie. They graciously invited their sisters, and then Collin stopped to pick up Franco, his friend's older brother. "No, not Franco!" Giancarlo moaned. "He makes me crazy." "Yes, Franco," insisted Collin. Some stories were poignant, many hilarious. Collin had made no new memories for nine months, so these anecdotes brought him back to us for a few precious moments. I put the letters in a scrapbook and read them frequently.

Many other presents that year also remembered our boy through the symbolism of stars. My parents gave us a lighted cube with Collin's face etched into the glass and gave me a diamond star necklace. Kelly named a star "Collin's Star" and gave us a framed map showing its location in the Perseus constellation. Ed and the kids surprised me with a set of dishes, blue with a large yellow star in the center and smaller ones around the edge, that they had snuck off to paint every Saturday morning at the local pottery place while I slept in. On the underside of each piece they had neatly printed the pattern name, "Remembering Collin." Ed also gave me star earrings and a star ring. I made everyone sweatshirts with stars and Collin's signature and gave Ed a mug with pictures of all three kids. Dozens of other gifts, from wall plaques to angel figurines, sported stars.

I survived the holidays (we ignored New Year's) while tiptoeing around the elephant in the room, a huge emptiness with its arm around everyone. Collin was everywhere, and nowhere. As if sitting out a penalty, he could no longer participate, and the game just wasn't the same.

Twisters

*T*he holidays punch hard, but they wave from the calendar, so you know long in advance that the right hook is coming. You expect December 25 will be tough, so you steel your grief muscles and view in slow motion that T-Rex about to T-bone your car.

But grief tornadoes swoop down out of a clear sky without warning, no screaming clarion riveting your attention. When you wake up on August 22, you have no idea a paroxysm of grief is about to knock you off your feet and thrash and buffet your heart, then drop you on your head in Oz. Over many months, you may manage to dig a storm shelter, but periodically the wind will rip the doors off and the rain will pour in while the monkeys fly by and laugh.

My first grief tornado touched down that first May in my local K-Mart, where I had gone to buy a birthday card for Collin. The greeting cards were immediately to my left as I entered the store. I found the birthday/son section and began pulling cards from the rack. Immediately I teared up. Each card triggered more tears, until I could no longer read the words. Determined to choose a card, I wiped my eyes, but it was no use. Sobbing, I stuffed the cards back into the display and careered out into the main aisle, narrowly missing a loaded shopping cart. Blindly, I ran. When I finally stopped, the first thing I saw was a mannequin dressed in a Henley shirt, Collin's signature fashion. I have no idea how I made it back to my car.

Another tornado hit a few months later when I thought I was ready to do the grocery shopping. I wasn't prepared for the assailants who lay in wait throughout the store. In every aisle, Collin's favorite foods attacked from the shelves—Kraft macaroni and cheese, Sprite, English muffins, Toblerone chocolate, ravioli, mozzarella sticks. . . . I abandoned my cart in the middle of the frozen foods.

The beach was Collin's (and my) happy place. When he was about ten, we purchased a mobile home just outside Rehoboth Beach. We went nearly every weekend, and sometimes the kids (and a half-dozen friends) and I stayed down for a week at a time. Collin loved to dig up sand crabs and catch sand sharks and ride the waves on his boogie board. He and his friends hopped the bus two miles into Rehoboth to play for prize tickets at the Dolles Arcade, twirl on the rides at Funland, and gorge on Grotto's pizza, Fisher's caramel corn, and Candy Kitchen sweets. Collin's presence was everywhere in our beach house. The sheets and comforter in the boys' bedroom sported images of all the Major League Baseball teams. Matt and Collin had decorated lockers with decals of their favorite sports team logos.

The first time we visited the beach house after Collin died, his trophies saluted from atop his locker. His boogie board waited in the closet. The nightstand drawer burst with baseball cards and Funland and Dolles Arcade tickets. In the living room, Collin's Uno cards itched for a game. Atop the baker's rack in the kitchen sat the framed recipe for chocolate chip cookies that Collin and Katie had bought at a neighborhood yard sale the first day we moved in. Their other purchase, a dried flower and grapevine wreath, hung on the wall in Ed's and my bedroom. To this day, I get a pang every time I see it. And Collin's swimsuit and baseball towel hung from pegs on the wooden shark on the bathroom wall. Because of his fascination with the creatures, I had stenciled huge sharks on Collin's bedroom wall at home when he was about six. He knew the names of every shark. I bought the bathroom shark with Collin in mind.

When we stepped foot on the sand, Collin was everywhere too. Every skinny blond boy with a droopy swimsuit caught my eye. Every teen riding a wave became my son. I jerked my head at every laugh, every screech.

Another grief tornado struck the day of my cousins' son's wedding. I had expected the day to be challenging, as it was always hard to smile and make small talk in social situations. But I never expected I wouldn't even make it to the event. That morning, I was seized by panic and paralysis. Instead of getting dressed and doing my makeup, I hyperventilated and broke out into a sweat. My heart pounded. I could not make my body move to get ready. The prospect of being in the presence of so much joy was a boulder teetering on a cliff over my head. We would never attend Collin's wedding.

Many other mini-storms touched down, jolting me from my illusion of control. Hearing "Forever Young" on the car radio, finding a Reese's Collin had hidden in the back of the fridge, eating mint chocolate chip ice cream, receiving an invitation to a graduation party, walking through the backyard blanketed with spring's tiny white flowers, seeing a teen in shorts and flip-flops in December. . . . Surprises like these triggered cascades of memories that left me bereft and hollow.

Although they still packed a punch, such surprises eventually lost their power to incapacitate, as each vaccinated me against future triggers. But for a long time, new ones continued to catch me unawares, keeping me on a roller coaster of emotion. Even today, if my guard is down, a grief tornado sometimes sweeps me off my composure.

The holidays were tough and grief tornadoes took their toll, but worst of all were the weeks that led up to the one-year anniversary of Collin's death. March was like an extended version of our hospital vigil. That we already knew the outcome made no difference.

For nine months, Grief had stomped on me and tossed me around like a rag doll. Then in January and February, it stepped back, letting me think it was easing. I breathed again. But in March it returned, crueler than ever, kidnapping me and holding me hostage from life. It tortured me more each day, and paralyzed, I floated like a wraith, observing but not participating. I perseverated even more than normal, unable to move from one task to another. As if relief might be found on the next webpage, I followed random threads on the internet, compulsively clicking link after link long after they offered anything of interest. I couldn't make myself step out of the shower until the water turned icy. I spent long days in Collin's room.

My thoughts, which always bombarded me like email spam, went into overdrive—*what if, if only, why didn't I, WHY?* I had managed not to dwell on these for months, but now such questions were all I could think of. And the tears I thought had diminished had only been collecting, waiting for March to pour out.

The tension built each week, until it was March 25. At 5:30 p.m., that awful phone call played in my mind as if on a loop. I was transported back to Christiana Hospital—pacing as I waited for the neurosurgeon to arrive, gasping in horror at the extent of Collin's injuries, sobbing with Ed in the hallway. Reality disappeared and the next four days got progressively worse, as my mind replayed the drama of the cranial pressure monitor, the brain scan, the callous bedside manner of the resident. Then it was the 30th, and I relived the surreal moment of Collin's death and the horror of the organ donation interview.

I wanted to do something to honor Collin's life and acknowledge the depth of our sorrow. All through March, through tears, I researched poems and songs and developed a memorial ceremony. On the 30th, our extended family joined us at the cemetery where we shared tributes and memories.

Four candles represented our grief and pain, our memories, our love, and Collin's immortality in the universe and in our hearts. As a group, we recited the Shakespeare verse on Collin's headstone. Next we took turns reading Byron, Shelley, Thoreau, Gibran, Gandhi, Saint-Exupery, and others. I particularly liked a line from novelist and war correspondent Larry Barretto: "Babies are bits of stardust blown from the hand of God. Lucky the woman who knows the pangs of birth, for she has held a star." My favorite was a poem written by Ralph Waldo Emerson after his son's death:

The South wind brings
Life, sunshine and desire
But over the dead he has no power,
The lost, the lost he cannot restore;
And looking over the hills, I mourn
The darling who shall not return.
. . . the deep-eyed boy is gone . . .

Our deep-eyed boy was gone.

Kelly reflected on the past year in a poem she wrote that began and ended, "One year today, / So hard to believe." She thanked Collin for everything his life and death taught us:

Thank you, Collin . . .
For a year of realization
That loving relationships are the most precious thing we can aspire to.
For a year of learning the true meaning of the gift of life.

I memorialized Collin in an original poem that ended:

Beautiful spirit,
Speed to eternity on the wings of our tears.
Look in on us now and then
And line our way with floodlights of love
That, when we follow, we will find the surest route.

We consoled ourselves with music—Boyz II Men's "It's So Hard to Say Goodbye to Yesterday," "I'll Back You Up" by the Dave Matthews Band, Wynonna's "You Were Loved," and "Angel" by Sarah McLachlan. There were tears and laughter as we shared Collin memories, and then we released balloons (we didn't know then how dangerous this is for wildlife). Afterward, we had all of Collin's favorites for dinner at our house. It was a poignant experience and helped us reset after our grief had ratcheted up all through March.

We did similar ceremonies every year for a decade. Sometimes we added experiences, like going to an Aberdeen Iron Birds[22] game or a stage play of *Monty Python and the Holy Grail*, painting more star dishes at the pottery place, or designing picture frames to display our Collin photos.

One year we played a Jeopardy game that featured lines from Collin's favorite movies—*Spaceballs, Animal House, Christmas Vacation, The Sandlot, Major League, Ghostbusters, Hot Shots Part Deux, History of the World Part I,* and *Groundhog Day* (these tell you a lot about Collin's sense of humor). Here's a sample:

---

[22] The Baltimore Orioles' minor league team.

Answer—"If that cat had nine lives, it sure used them all" *(Christmas Vacation)*.

Question—Who was Collin's cat, Sparckey?

Graduation Grace

We hadn't planned to attend Collin's high school graduation, as he died in the spring of his junior year. But here we were—my parents, Matt, Katie, Ed, and me—a bubble of despair shielding us from hugs, congratulations, and the "empires of the future"[23] that floated around the auditorium.

From the moment we entered the arena, I realized it would be worse than I had pictured. It was torturous to watch other families celebrate their children's accomplishments and look ahead to college or careers, knowing that no future awaited our son. A few friends greeted us, but their wide eyes and frozen smiles made me avoid eye contact with anyone else as we found our way to reserved seats to the left of the dais. It seemed an eternity before "Pomp and Circumstance" blared over the speakers, and young women in blue and young men in green, robes flowing and smiles glowing, marched in.

We listened to welcomes and speeches by the principal, the president of the school board, student leaders, and U. S. Senator Joe Biden.

When we were called onstage, I could hardly walk and held Ed's arm to keep myself steady. The principal announced that a dogwood tree would be planted in front of the school in Collin's memory, along with a plaque with his name on it. He handed us Collin's diploma.

---

[23] "The empires of the future are the empires of the mind." —Winston Churchill

As we made our way off the stage, I felt an urge to veer off to the podium to address the crowd. Instead, tears flooded my vision, and I stumbled back to my seat. I have always regretted that I didn't take advantage of that spontaneous moment to share my son's legacy with his peers. Here's what I wish I had said:

My family and I weren't planning to come tonight. As you might imagine, it has been difficult to witness so much joy while we are consumed with grief. But Mr. Keister said the class wanted to present us with a diploma for Collin. Then we learned you planned a memorial to him, and it felt like someone—God? the universe? Collin?—desperately wanted us to be here. We wanted to personally accept your generous gifts. Thank you for remembering Collin in this way.

I wasn't asked to speak and did not prepare remarks. But as I listened to the administrators, the student leaders, and Senator Biden, it dawned on me why I was here—not just to accept your gift *to* Collin, but to deliver a message *from* him. I hope you will grant a bereaved mother a few moments' grace to talk to you.

Graduates, every single speaker gushed about the promise of the future and focused on the same theme—never give up. Each exhorted you to persevere in whatever field you choose—that you must give your all even when the way seems impossible, that the only failure is in quitting before achieving your goals, and that hard work will pay off in the end.

In this world of crazy coincidences (or synchronicities), it just so happens that this was Collin's mantra—Never Give Up. He once wrote an essay about his admiration for Orioles baseball player Cal Ripken, who never gave up "despite insurmountable odds."

Some of you may know that Collin had Tourette Syndrome, a neurological condition that causes physical and vocal tics, along with associated conditions such as ADHD and depression. Collin was embarrassed by tics. He was bullied by those who, incorrectly, assumed he was intellectually disabled. He struggled with depression as we tried one medicine after another. But through it all, Collin never gave up. He found his way through the darkness, and his junior year brought enormous positive changes. His depression lifted. He learned to drive and got a job

134

(and a promotion) at Best Buy. He earned a spot as WMCK's sports editor, worked as an aide for his chemistry teacher, and made the honor roll, the baseball team, and new friends.

So I believe the universe and Collin conspired to bring me here today to echo the words of your distinguished speakers. Although his life was short, Collin lived it to the fullest. He overcame his challenges and worked toward achieving his dream of being a sports commentator. I hope you will think of Collin in moments when your obstacles seem insurmountable as well as when you feel the thrill of triumph. Follow his example to you, his classmates—never give up.

Thank you.

When the graduation ceremony concluded, Senator Biden came over to us and offered condolences on our loss. Then he turned to thirteen-year-old Katie and they had a *tête-à-tête* for several minutes. He asked how Matt and she were doing, then told her about his own family's loss.[24] He shared his dad's best advice—if life knocks you down, get back up. We were impressed by his compassion in spending so much time with someone who wouldn't be eligible to vote for years while hundreds of active constituents waited to bend his ear.

---

[24] Shortly after his election to the U.S. Senate in 1972, Biden's wife and baby daughter were killed in a car accident. His two sons were injured, and he was sworn in next to their hospital beds.

135

March Madness

March is when I do the "what ifs," the "coulda, woulda, shouldas," the "if onlys," the "whys." Spit at a god I don't believe in. Wish for a slap in the face that would spin the earth clockwise and wake me. We should be able to abandon a world in which children die. I consider afterlife travel plans and wonder how far ahead one must book.

March is when I wrestle with all the demons I try to ignore the rest of the year.

Collin, your accident plays over and over on my mind's screen like a SciFi horror movie marathon. The pressure in my chest returns for this new vigil as if the heart-crushing monster from Mars is pleased to perform its recurring cameo. From a paper grocery bag in the back of my closet I take the clothes the paramedics cut off you—the khaki pants, the navy Henley shirt, the black knit Jockey boxers, the black Reebok sneakers—and press them to my face. They still hold your scent! Or is it just that I want it to be so? The fabric is stiff in places where blood soaked your shirt. I can touch it even though I cannot see it. I discover a fresh well of tears and marvel that any remain.

March is when I imagine how you'd look today. Taller, surely; shoulders broader than Batman's; muscles toned from baseball workouts. The blond you insisted was never in your hair would have gone almost totally to brown, and you'd sport a short, military cut. Stubble would dot your square jaw and inch up still-ruddy cheeks, having replaced every speck of baby fat. Two things would be just as

I remember—your eyes would still glint like holograms, with mischief and wonder and sadness all at once; and your smile would contain its own sun.

March is when I reflect upon the boy who nearly reached adulthood but will never know a man's joys. You should have managed the radio station and danced at the prom; known the freedom of a dorm and complained about the food. You, who predicted Mark McGwire's ascent, should have cheered his triumphant home run circuit. And after your first vote, your boos should have echoed to Florida and the Supreme Court. You should have kissed a girl, gotten drunk, gotten laid—fallen in love and planned a future to include children who grow up. How would your dreams have changed? How cruel that a boy who conquered "seemingly insurmountable obstacles" will never again know challenge.

March is when I adore friends who say your name and scowl at those who would rather die than mention you. I long for a new story about you, a just-remembered anecdote, an updated photo—but you create no new memories.

March is when I crawl through a tunnel with only dark at the end, rock scraping my belly and back, the air stale as it rushes to desert me. Still I can't let the lion or the lamb pass unremarked.

March is when we die again and again, the two of us.

If Only . . .

I don't generally wallow in the futile illusion of "if onlys." Nothing can change what has already happened, so there is little use in fantasizing about a do-over. But I am bowled over by the sheer number of events and decisions that produced the perfect storm of Collin's accident and eventual death.

★ If only it had rained that day, or snowed. Instead, spring arrived early wearing all its finery, exhorting us to throw off winter's baggage and revel in the sun's lapsed caress.

★ If only Coach had made sure Collin got the right-sized jersey, our son would have been hitting baseballs in Glasgow instead of shooting baskets at home in Hockessin. No "but"—Coach gets an error here.

★ If only our family preferred baseball to basketball. Except that we do, through and through. When I offered to sign up four-year-old Matt for soccer, he glared at me, hands on hips: "Mom! We're a baseball family!" It wasn't enough to love baseball. We needed to hate basketball.

★ If only we had never put up that basketball hoop. Now rusting with torn netting, it swallows occasional bank shots by Ed and our niece Maggie while it waits for the grandchildren's growth spurts. But I hate it—hate how it looms there a silent, mocking reminder.

★ If only Ed had worked late that day, maybe there would have been no pickup game. But aren't such joyful interactions the whole point of life? I just wish everyone had come inside immediately.

★ If only I hadn't stayed after school to lead a computer workshop, I might have made dinner while they performed pump fakes and pick and rolls, and Collin would have come inside rather than crossing the street with Pat. But I'm cursed with the need to educate others—it's encoded in my DNA.

★ If only someone who lived on our street had been the friend playing ball that day, instead of Patrick, who drove here. There would have been no car to jump on. But Patrick was Collin's first new friend in ages, and he was excited to spend time with him.

★ If only Patrick had gone right home, rather than fooling around with Collin. But it was Collin who jumped on the hood of his car.

★ If only Collin hadn't been holding a Sprite when he jumped on the hood of Patrick's car, maybe he wouldn't have lost his grip. But who doesn't quench his thirst after a lively pickup game?

★ If only Collin had never been introduced to hood surfing. But he never expected to fall, or to die. We had no intimation of the land mine poised to explode in Collin's brain, its flak spraying extracorporeally to pierce all our hearts.

★ If only we had never moved to Mendenhall Village. But all three kids raved about growing up there, spending unfettered summers outdoors and nurturing lifelong friendships.

★ If only Collin had never met Patrick. No—I would never deny him the grace of friendship.

If even *one* of these events hadn't occurred, Collin might still be alive. But such musings are no comfort. Even if none had come to pass, would he have died a different day in a different way?

VI
Book of Tears

*Perhaps the oceans
comprise the salty tears
wept by grieving mothers.*

Barometer

*G*rief is the barometer of my love. As one is intense and all-consuming, so is the other. Not to mourn would be not to love, and perhaps to lose the tether that connects us. Grief is not a puddle to vault. It is to roll in, inhale, taste—whether clover or compost, Emeraude or effluvium. Grief must be felt, listened to, cajoled, bargained with, attended to. Most of all, felt. Intensely.

Life is sensate. Perhaps there is a grace in feeling not generic happiness and sadness but the polar extremes of ecstasy and despair. And as psychiatrist Leonard M. Zunin wrote in *The Art of Condolence,* "Grief is the way the psyche heals itself." To deny grief is to refuse the heart-salve it offers as condolence for irrevocable loss—like refusing to put iodine on a cut because it might sting.

"Consolation and comfort are to be found where our wounds hurt most," Dutch priest Henri J. M. Nouwen wrote to his father. Beyond balm, grief brings consolation prizes— introspection and insight and perspective and humility, which allow us to peer over the ledge of spirit while keeping our tippy-toes grounded in earthly sensation.

Journal

April 7, 1998

It's been a week now since Collin died. I just took Katie back to school. Matt is working with his dad. Here at home it's quiet and still, just the dogs and cats and me. The emptiness and sadness are profound. I'm crying again, after just feeling blank yesterday. Nothing seems important. Doing things for Katie and Matt are the only things able to get me moving. Even then, everything is in slow motion and requires great effort.

This journal arrived today, a gift from the family of one of my nicest students. I wasn't sure I could write in it—didn't know if I could handle the emotions, if I could make the words make sense—but after I set it aside on the counter, something drew me back. I'm much more attuned to coincidences and signs now, so maybe this, too, is Collin's gentle puppeteering. Writing has always been cathartic for me and he's making sure I get this help.

April 11, 1998

How might things be different if I'd followed my heart? If I'd stayed home to raise you instead of buying a new house? If I'd said the hell with Highlands School and come home to you earlier each day? If we'd moved away to a calmer, less hectic life?

I told myself I wouldn't do the "what ifs," but it's hard. What if I'd been home earlier that day—maybe you'd have been eating dinner instead of jumping on Patrick's car. What if we'd never moved here? What if I'd swallowed my gigantic hubris and let you talk on and on when you gushed about something? What if I'd never fussed at you for your messy room? What if I'd been more sympathetic when depression clutched you or your stomach lurched or your head ached? It's awful to think that my doing one thing differently might have changed your course.

April 16, 1998

I saw you everywhere today, sweet boy. Someone sitting on a bench in the park looked like you from the back, and my heart stopped. I saw a red Prelude like yours, saw a *South Park* cartoon, saw your juice cans in the fridge. I saw little kids and thought of you, and saw teenagers booming by in their cars and thought of you. I deposited your final paycheck and sorted your mail from colleges. You're everywhere, and I want it to comfort me, but it doesn't.

April 26, 1998

I feel so old, as if I've skipped adulthood and gone right to old age. You're not supposed to feel this loneliness and despair until then. You're not supposed to bury your children.

April 30, 1998

Today was the first day I've felt okay about going to your grave. I cut some lilacs and a big tree peony and took them. I tidied things up, and culled the dead parts of the old flowers. It gave me a sense of ease to make things look nice for you. It's still hard to see that tiny patch of ground and think of you under there, all still, all alone. I said to you, "I guess it's like you've gotten sent to your room for forever." I know you smiled.

May 4, 1998

Oh, Collin. I thought maybe I'd be okay today. I got up to take Katie to school and then cleaned a bit and read the paper and took a shower. But I don't feel like doing anything else except being sad. I just want to sit here on your bed and write and cry and think about you. I have, in a shopping bag in my closet, the clothes you wore when you got hurt. They're all tattered, since the EMTs cut them off you. Yesterday I smelled your shirt again. I could smell your sweat and I cried, envisioning you lying in the street, hurting and sweating. Your shirt was navy blue, so it's hard to see the blood. Still, you can smell its metallic odor, and it's hardened, so you can feel where it is. . . . I know it's stupid, but I want to write, "Why did you die? Where are you? When are you coming back?"

May 9, 1998

I'm being selfish today. Tough. As your third-grade teacher used to say, "Too bad, so sad." Tomorrow is Mother's Day and I'm supposed to have my kids—all of them. You were my Mother's Day baby—I labored all day and had you early the next morning—and I always considered it magical serendipity. Now I can't decide whether your connection with Mother's Day is a blessing, because you made that holiday singularly significant, or a curse, because you'll never again be here to help me celebrate it.

August 9, 1998

Now there are only four people in our family. I always knew we were five, never counted. If Mom Mom and Pop Pop joined us for dinner, I thought *five plus two*. Now, I have to count heads when figuring out how many dinner places to set, how many seats to ask for at a restaurant. I don't automatically think *four plus extras*. If Grammy and Grandfather come over, I think *one, two, three, four plus two*. I think I just can't believe we are only four now. And we don't know where to sit at dinner either. Should Katie get your seat now? Or Matt? Or should we leave it ever empty?

September 1, 1998

I read in a book about a woman who cried for two days because she forgot the sound of her husband's voice. Will I forget how your voice sounds? Right now, it's clear to me. I hear you say, "Hey, Mom," hear your laugh, hear you getting excited about something, cussing at the video games. I might cry for two days, too, if I lost that precious sound. I guess I'll always be able to visualize you from your pictures. I can still remember how your skin felt and how it felt when I hugged you or touched your hair. Will I lose those?

I guess I don't quite understand why people try to fight grief—put on a brave front, lose themselves in work, pretend things are normal. Grief is my friend, my protection, my defense. I need it. I want it. When I am ready, it will fade. But if I try to deny it, it will hide to leap out and frighten me when I least expect it.

Oh, Sweetie. Every time I turn on the computer, I see your files. When I fire up the internet, there's "Collin's Excite Page." You were forever changing things and then my stuff wouldn't work right. Well, now, the computer is always the same as I left it. Everything works and I hate it. The scissors are always in the drawer and I hate it. The American cheese lasts for days. There are no more Hershey's kisses hidden in the produce drawer. No one drives the Prelude. There's no one to sell me on the latest infomercial. I hate signing cards without your name. I hate it all.

September 23, 1998

I do well when things are calm and I have no commitments or responsibilities. But I'm only good because I'm numb, out of the loop. I can be alive, but I can't live. I don't cry much around others, and I guess they think I'm doing well, but to me, it just seems so intimate to cry. I don't want to share it with anyone.

The Bad Mother

I always prided myself on being a good mother. Yes, I lost my temper sometimes and yelled at my kids and spanked them when they misbehaved (until Dr. W. told us about timeouts). But it was the eighties and so did everyone we knew. Ed was a good father, and we tried to maintain a united front as we parented as a team and modeled our values. We held our children to high standards of behavior, respect, and character and trained them to be independent. We made them do chores, which led to innumerable Collin rants and timeouts. Our children can list our faults, but we always did the best we could and worked to be consistent and fair, despite Collin's TS.

What I am most proud of is that we not only loved our children, we enjoyed being with them. Everyone played at our house. When other parents dreaded the end of school in June, we rejoiced. Whole days to do fun things together! We spent afternoons at the pool, took day trips to the beach, discovered museums and aquariums, visited nearby cities, played board games, screamed at amusement parks, ate too much junk food at local fairs and festivals, checked out historic sites, went tent camping. Even when we just stayed home, Ed and I loved to sit on the porch and watch and listen to the kids playing in the yard with their friends.

Then Collin died, and that mom died too. Along with my son, I lost all sense of who I was, my energy, and my *joie de vivre*. Like Ukranian *pysanky*[25] Easter eggs, I was hollow, my essence—my soul—blown away. Our adventures ceased. I became that movie stereotype of the depressed mother who drinks and takes pills and lives in bed. Except that my only drug was grief. It kept me under its thumb, possessed me, dictated every movement, every emotion. It filled my days with itself so no other sensory input could enter. I couldn't fall asleep at night and couldn't get up in the morning. At night, no one makes demands of you. When you're asleep, no one wants to wake you. So I became a vampire and shunned the sun, switching day and night to avoid interacting with anyone. I never actually planned this, and only realized the causality much later.

I wanted to disappear. Sometimes I wondered if I should be hospitalized, although I never shared this fear with anyone. My family didn't need one more thing to worry about, and I didn't need them tiptoeing around me wondering if my next mini-breakdown was *the one*. I withdrew from everyone and wrapped myself in a cocoon of nothingness lest the weight of the world would crumble me to dust. Life reeled in exaggerated slow motion as few activities filled the time. Someone must have tossed clothes into the washer when we ran out of underwear or run the vacuum when the doggie tumbleweeds got too high to wade through, but I don't remember doing any of it. Since I was usually in Collin's room crying late in the day, Ed fixed dinner (after working all day, bless him), and all of us did manage to eat together.

I was too out of it to feel guilty about neglecting my family, but honestly, no one seemed to miss me. We all pulled away from attention as if it burned. My family had donned their own armor—Katie listened to music in her room, Matt slept all day in his, and Ed disappeared into the TV like Carol Anne in *Poltergeist*. Rejecting any intrusion into their solitude, they processed grief in their own ways. We made Matt and Katie go to a sibling grief workshop, which they hated. When I tried to initiate conversations about what happened and how they felt, they said they didn't want to talk about it. This was strange, since we had always talked through our problems before, one child or another perched on the kitchen counter bewailing the end of a romance, a teacher who was unfair, a friend who had been unkind.

---

[25] *Pysanky* are Easter eggs decorated with intricate Ukrainian folk designs. Before they are painted, the artist pokes holes in each end and blows out the insides.

Eventually, chinks appeared in the armor. I helped Katie deal with crumbling friendships and uncomfortable situations at school. I hooked her up with a therapist and commiserated as she struggled with her flute solos. I counseled Matt on how to get a second chance in college and helped him find a mortgage and move into his new house.

We each needed to find our own way. If Katie's friends were assholes, she needed to find new ones. If Matt needed to sleep his grief, then he could go back to school when things were better. I was there when they reached out, but I am ashamed that I wasn't able to push aside my own troubles to be proactive for my kids, to be the one who reached out to them. I will forever regret that at the moment they were most vulnerable, I let them down. I would have died for my children, but I couldn't find a way to live for them. Because she was young, Katie needed me, so she and I stayed close, but Matt learned to live without me, and our relationship has never been the same.

VII
Boxing with Oz

All-knowing, all-loving (?), all-powerful God—
You're nothing but a selfish bully,
A munchkin hustling behind a curtain
Pretending to be the great and powerful
Oz . . .

Flight Path

*T*wo-and-a-half years after Collin died, things had settled into a routine. I still slept poorly and visited the cemetery frequently but no longer spent all day in Collin's room. Although grief tornadoes still swept me up at times, I was more empty than sad. I was ready to push myself to do more but filled with dread at the thought of staying upbeat and smiling while managing hundreds of demands a day teaching young children. I missed the kids, missed the creative work of teaching, but it was exhausting on a good day, and I knew I didn't have enough cans of Popeye's emotional spinach to survive it.

Learning had always been effortless for me, so I took the easier path and headed back to school as a student, rather than a teacher, pursuing a master's degree in creative writing. Sitting passively in class and doing readings were no trouble. The writing work challenged and demanded in its own way, but I could complete assignments at my own pace. If Monday was Cryday, I wrote my paper on Tuesday. Plus, I could choose what to write about, and I chose to write about Collin. Many nights I cried at the computer, but addressing my grief helped me corral it. My thesis was the kernel for this book.

After graduation, I was asked to stay on as an instructor, teaching composition and argument. I was excited to be back at teaching but relieved it was at a slower pace. Twice a week, I taught for an hour-and-a-half and went home, then graded papers and planned lessons when I felt up to it. I eventually took responsibility for more classes, at times teaching creative writing, composition, or speech and presentation at two different universities. The students were enthusiastic and endearing, and I loved watching their writing—and themselves—blossom. I limited my load to two or three classes a semester, more because of the piles of papers to grade than the calm, pleasant teaching time. One semester I taught five classes and nearly had a breakdown.

Collin had been gone five years, and life was busy again. It wasn't that I had a ton of things to do, but I wasn't sitting around watching soaps and eating bonbons. Mainly I took care of my family, did chores, and taught classes. I did ten times that before Collin died, and I thrived on the adrenalin. But there was no climate change inside me. My grief loomed large every day, just under the surface, and that iceberg wasn't melting any time soon. I swam hard to keep afloat. It was as if I breast-stroked with fifty pounds strapped to my back, and one more ounce of stress could pull me down.

When that happened, my life became the bonbons from that *I Love Lucy* candy assembly line scene. The chocolates kept coming and coming and piled up and piled up. Lucy and Ethel stuffed the boxes faster and faster, but candy continued to spill onto the floor. Finally they started stuffing them into their mouths to keep up. Except my bonbon scenes didn't feel funny.

I only survived because I strictly regulated my responsibilities, stressors, and interactions. I learned to manage my grief the way Collin handled his Tourette's—holding it at bay when I needed to and then letting it out when it was safe. I smiled and brushed my hair and went to the Acme and graded essays and cooked dinner, but I didn't accept new commitments or make social plans. On the days I didn't teach, I slept late. If I wasn't up to vacuuming, I didn't.

Sometimes it feels like I've been having a breakdown for twenty years. But somewhere between five and seven years after Collin died, I felt a lightening, as if some of the fifty-pound weight had fallen away. My grief still leered at me, but it didn't try to drown me every day. Physically, I could move better and be more active.

Since then, the weight has continued to dissolve, and I've made it to shore, so now I navigate my days carrying only about twenty-five pounds in boxes on my shoulders that I can never put it down. Along with the seventy pounds I've gained on my own, Grief lets me know who is still in charge.

Impossible Optimism

*D*reams get crushed all the time. She doesn't get accepted to Harvard; he loses the election for president. She can't get pregnant; he'll never be tall enough to play for the Philadelphia 76ers. Most adapt. She goes to Yale; he becomes the Senate Foreign Affairs Committee Chair. She adopts; he organizes a basketball league for players under six feet tall with new rules that draw fans in droves. We are an adaptive species. When plan A falls apart like one of Wile E. Coyote's Acme Roadrunner-catching gadgets, we go to plan B. Sometimes plan B leads to a better consequence than plan A might ever have. My husband, for example, would never have launched his own successful business had he not been fired from a previous job.

I used to inspire my students with a quote from Thomas Edison: "I haven't failed. I've found 10,000 ways that don't work." Everything is possible, fixable. That worked great for the third-grader who struggled with sentence fragments or the one whose Rube Goldberg contraption fell to pieces during the bus ride to school. Even what seems impossible, like beaming from place to place à la Star Trek or becoming invisible, may someday come to pass—it's just a matter of conquering the science. A little over a century ago, no one believed people would ever fly. Just a couple of decades ago, no one imagined we would find a way to print human organs. In 2018, researchers in Montreal used "spectral cloaking" to hide objects from broadband light.

This belief in possibility leads to amazing optimism. Incredible advances are made by those who refuse to accept "it's impossible" as a limitation. Optimists are giddy with the delusion that life is within their control. I was one of those idealists.

But death is the one area that belies such belief. Intellectually, we can predict that science will one day discover the fountain of youth, learn to reanimate corpses, or open the portal (within ourselves or at some external access point) to connect life with afterlife. Architect Stephen Valentine designed the Timeship, a six-acre "Noah's Ark" dedicated to cryonically preserving species for a more technologically-advanced future, and psychic Sylvia Browne claims to have visited the "other side." But does anyone expect that, in our lifetime, deceased loved ones will reappear and go on with life?

No matter what I do, what I try, how I persevere, how much I spend, how many tears I cry, I cannot bring my son back to life. It is beyond my control. It is impossible.

Such an admission is painful for an optimist. After the agony of missing my son, this is the side effect of death I find most difficult to live with. *It is impossible* has caused sadness and depression, emptiness and hopelessness. It has also evoked a sense of betrayal, which is the closest my grief has come to generating true anger.

Optimists operate under a naïve, yet workable credo that you create your own destiny, inviting positive outcomes and avoiding negative ones through targeted effort and careful planning. Until 1998, this worked well for me. Good grades, creative ideas, and careful deliberation led to a successful career in education. Family planning and consistent saving helped my husband and me buy our first home. Targeted observation and research helped us create a loving, nurturing atmosphere for our children. I assumed an unwritten rule that attuning my behavior to the golden rule afforded golden-fleece protection against adversity.

Then my son died through no one's fault, and my assumptions laughed in my face: "Control? Are you kidding?" The cruel betrayal seeped into all areas of my life.

Through experiments with rats, psychologist B. F. Skinner showed that when rewarded regularly for an action, rats learn to repeat it. When shocked, they swiftly avoid that conduct. When reward and punishment are inconsistent, rats may continue the action, but will exhibit neurotic or psychotic behaviors.

People aren't so different from rats.

Like the rats', my trust has been compromised and I can't identify the source of my betrayal or its motivations. Whether by God, the universe, or accident, my spirit has been quashed. This double cross has also made me hypersensitive to other betrayals.

Friends betray, unable or unwilling to share grief's enormous pain. Their eyes glaze during the eighty-seventh rehash of the "if onlys." They pout that I haven't returned their calls or invited them over—after all, it's long past my turn. Squirming at the threat of tears, they don't speak Collin's name for fear the menace will manifest. To assuage their own discomfort, they employ guerilla tactics to eradicate, if not grief itself, at least its incarnations. Heartwarming stories about others who have "conquered" their grief are thinly-veiled hints that it is time to move on. All the old activities they miss—shopping, dancing, holding riveting conversations—would be "good" for me, they insist, clucking that hiding in bed crying means I am not trying to get better. They pounce on any hint of improvement—a stray smile, combed hair, a lucid dialogue—as evidence that mourning is—whew!—ending, and reinforce the moment as if I were a child to be manipulated into proper behavior. I'll just say that anyone who doesn't understand why I can't move on should be grateful.

Religion betrays, offering nothing but the promise of faith for one whose faith has crumbled into so much kibble. For a firm believer, faith is a comfort. For the ambivalent, the Christmas-and-Easter Catholic, it is a lure that dangles just beyond reach. Just when I most need the support of fellowship, the counsel of learned teachers, and the balm of ritual, questions and doubt make me a heretic, sending me to psychics and mediums for answers and reassurance. Sermons that tout God's love become spiteful jabs. Hymns that proclaim "Praise God, from whom all blessings flow" choke.

Fire and brimstone approaches can be even worse. At my uncle's funeral, the preacher never said anything about him except, "Arthur died because he was a sinner." He went on to declare stillborn babies sinners. Even though I recognized original sin as the scriptural basis for the preacher's rantings, I took offense at his implication that my sixteen-year-old, who hadn't lived long enough to do anything awful, was a sinner. Many of my relatives marched out in protest. I stayed, so flabbergasted that I wanted to hear what other invectives he planned to voice. I later confronted him and told him how much his words had hurt.

Society betrays when it relegates the deceased's name to the realm of four-letter-words and expects the bereaved to hide their pain and return almost immediately to daily routines. The disability insurance I had paid into for fifteen years covered only two years for a mental illness, although my grief carried on unabated. In fact, grief itself was not covered at all—my condition had to be listed as major depression. Fortunately, the state awarded me a disability pension.

Even institutions committed to comforting the bereaved betray. The cemetery where we buried Collin rejected the Shakespeare quotation we had chosen to engrave on his headstone. "When he shall die, take him and cut him out in little stars, and he will make the face of heaven so fine that all the world will be in love with night and pay no worship to the garish sun" was blasphemous, but Disney lyrics and images of Harley-Davidsons and race cars were fine. We appealed and won. When, after more than a year, we hadn't heard from any of Collin's recipients, we suggested that the organ donation organization urge recipients to send timely thank you notes to donors' families. They rejected our suggestion. A grief support group we attended frowned on expressions of sorrow and hopelessness, even though such venting was what my husband and I (at least, I) most needed.

Finally, my own body betrays me, laying down dead-end memory circuits and clouding perception. It insists on unnatural amounts of sleep or disallows it altogether. And it refuses to release the energy I attempt to fuel with countless carbohydrates, hoarding it because of course I need to drag around a hundred extra pounds of dead weight.

None of it seems fair. Sometimes at the cemetery, I scream that to the crows, along with FUCKFUCKFUCK! The betrayals erode trust, exploding like boils. Cynicism that nothing can be predicted or controlled and people will always look out for themselves first and care most about superficial issues eats away hope like a malignancy, and anger simmers just beneath my skin. Yet my anger is contained by the realization that it will be of no consequence to any but me.

Anger?

*A*nger. Such a straightforward, honest feeling. There's never any equivocating about whether someone is angry or toward whom it is focused. Babies as young as three-and-a-half months can recognize anger. It is possibly the emotion most difficult to hide from others, as the steam builds and is vented in little puffs visible as narrowed eyes, clenched fists, or snappish behavior even before the main boiler blows.

Anger can even be predicted in certain situations. A wife betrayed will become angry. A teenager unjustly (or often, justly) punished will become angry. A parent whose daughter is raped will become angry. And a person who is mourning will become angry.

Anger is the second stage in death and grief expert Elisabeth Kübler-Ross' stages of grief, occurring after shock and denial and before bargaining, distress and despair, and acceptance and resignation. Although Kübler-Ross noted that the stages are fluid and may be experienced in a different order, she maintained that everyone who grieves will, at some point, experience each emotion.

Kübler-Ross's stages of grief theory has come under considerable attack from those in the field, but it makes common sense that losing a beloved might make someone boil with anger.

After my son Collin died, I experienced shock and denial, bargaining, and distress and despair. I kept waiting for anger. Twenty-two years later, I'm still waiting for that train. I've jumped ahead to Resignation Station.

It's not that anger and I aren't acquainted. I confronted a contractor who withheld $8000 he owed my husband. I've never again spoken to a woman who, while I was PTA president, went behind my back to push a pet initiative the executive board and principal had rejected. I got angry regularly, once throwing the Nintendo console across his room, when Collin reacted to any imposition with Tourette-induced rages. I was angry even over minor things—my husband passive-aggressively letting the dogs bark, the kids whining over cleaning their rooms.

But I haven't been angry—screaming, stomping, veins in the neck bulging, throwing the Nintendo angry—since Collin died.

There have been auditions. My best friend came to Collin's funeral and then didn't call for six months. Another friend so badgered me to get counseling that I stopped answering her calls. Someone we considered a friend betrayed our trust and exploited our daughter's vulnerability.

I've been unable to manage more than annoyance or disappointment toward any of them. After surviving a child, nothing else registers on the horror meter. But it's more than that. There's an element of futility now—anger doesn't accomplish anything—and I realize anger is an arduous attempt to gain the delusion of control. Anger won't bring Collin back. Beyond that, I am consumed by larger issues of God and the universe and the purpose of life. Anger won't provide those answers.

My child's death changed my beliefs about God and religion. I vacillated between two scenarios, each with endless variations: One, there must not be a God at all, because a loving God wouldn't cause such anguish; and two, God must not be that white-haired, bearded, kind old man who watches over us, but some organizing force, akin to gravity or electromagnetism, that created the world but doesn't direct it. In neither scenario is there anyone to blame.

Anger feeds on blame. Anger needs a conscious, unconscionable act to sink its teeth into, and in Collin's death, there wasn't one.

Some who grieve find themselves angry at the person who died, angry at being left alone, or angry at the inconsolable state the death cast them into. My Aunt Sal, whose police detective husband was murdered, shook her fist at the sky and yelled, "Damn you, Bob! Damn you for dying and leaving me!"

I still need intent. Collin didn't die on purpose to make me miserable. The action that took his life, falling from the hood of his friend's moving car, was just one more impulsive exploit—common in those with Tourette Syndrome—we had come to expect from Collin. Other kids did the same thing in the school parking lot. He never expected it to kill him, didn't know an aneurysm lurked in his brain. Moreover, Collin had just had one of the best afternoons ever and was showing off for the first new friend he had made since childhood. My Icarus flew too close to the sun. I would be selfish to be angry at such happiness.

Some people expect me to be angry at Patrick, the car's driver. After the accident, the police officer recommended that the boy not go to the hospital. Yet Patrick didn't initiate the situation. Collin ran out on his own and jumped on the hood.

Another target for my potential anger is Collin's baseball coach. On that March afternoon that belonged in early June, Collin should not have been home bouncing a basketball, but batting in the season's opening game. However, his uniform pants were too small. The coach said it was too late to sort it out and promised to set things straight before the next game. Sans uniform, Collin came home. Perhaps the coach should have better organized, or maybe he should have fixed things right away. But with the players dressed and ready to board the bus. . . . Collin wasn't even angry at missing the game. I'm not angry, either, but I confess to still holding a grudge over the coach's failure.

I've even tried being angry at myself—searched for a way to blame myself for my son's death. When the accident occurred around 5:30, I was still at school, cleaning up after showing other teachers how to load software onto their classroom computers. Ironically, Collin had unselfishly set up those computers the August before. But even invoking mother-guilt didn't work for me. Had I been home, I wouldn't have been outside monitoring Collin. Even standing right next to him, I couldn't have prevented his impulsive dash.

Maybe I should be angry that Collin had Tourette Syndrome, which likely precipitated his impulsive act. However, I spent that anger many Collin-rages ago.

That brings me back to God. Poems I've written seethe at God, but are complicated by indecision about my beliefs. I'm angry at a God I don't believe in. The sting lacks venom.

So I keep an anger vigil, waiting for the Vesuvius that may someday erupt despite my calm rationalization. For anger is, after all, neither rational nor calm. I wonder whether to cheer that I haven't experienced anger or to invite it—whether anger would be the key to assuage my grief or, as one more useless protest, exacerbate it.

Kahlil Gibran's words give pause: "If your heart is a volcano, how shall you expect flowers to bloom?" But even without anger, can flowers bloom in the toxic earth of grief?

No Deal

*G*od doesn't do eBay. Never cruises the antique lamps (he is *light,* after all) or drools over the Mark McGwire memorabilia *(I reserved the seventh day for rest, not "Play ball!").* Maybe he thinks haggling is beneath him *(It's $80. I'll give you $60. No, $80, firm as the commandment tablets.).* Or he just sees it as a joke—*Cosmic Comedy Central.* How he must cackle at us mortals, so self-possessed over the "blue round sunglasses like Ozzy or Lennon" we snagged for $6 or the "medieval armor Roman helmet" steal at $150.

Bottom line—God doesn't bargain. It's his way or the hellish highway. I have worked all the angels [sic] to get him to try it just once—to make a deal with me for my son's return. I'll take door number one, God. I'll trade it all for Collin behind the curtain. But God is no Monty Hall.

The Golden Rule thing is for suckers. God casts it out into the cosmos and leans back with a St. Pauli Girl to see how many naïve goody-goodies he can reel in. Fee-fi-fo-fum—he got me good. Legally, though, he's off the hook—had his lawyers draft the language. It's a real tour de force—doesn't even need fine print or legalese. The simple and straightforward language is deceptive: "Do unto others as you would have them do unto you." If you follow this doctrine, only good things will come, right? Wrong. This isn't dogma as much as dog-doo.

Same with the Ten Commandments. Our responsibilities are definite—literally cast in stone—but God's are vague, like eternity or houses with many rooms. He obviously wants us to follow his rules, so I thought a promise not to lie or steal or covet my neighbor's wife or make any graven images was a pretty good trade for my son's life. No deal.

What if I went above and beyond, then? Did extra good deeds? Ha! You know how at the Dollar Store everything is a dollar? At celestial customer service, everything is "No!"

How 'bout if I'm nice to my kids?

No.

I'll deliver meals to the homeless.

Forget it.

Join Mother Teresa's order and minister to the poor in Delhi.

Sure—one spider up your sari and you'll beg to renegotiate your deal.

Negotiate peace between Israel and the Palestinians.

Even I haven't been able to fix that hot mess.

I refused to fold without a fight. No wimp, I promised future good works: I'll gladly do a good deed Thursday if you send my son back today.

No deal, Wimpy.

Some shrewd negotiator, God. Must have eaten his spinach.

"Didn't you read our exchange policy?" asked a white-haired guy with plaid pants, a black shirt, and white patent-leather shoes. He pointed to a sign behind the counter he lounged against: "No returns, refunds, or exchanges. Ever. At any time. For any reason. This means you."

I had never missed K-Mart so much. Still, I tried. Tried to return the unused portion of my life for a store credit. Tried to get a refund on the life that wasn't as advertised. Tried to exchange my life for Collin's.

"I'll give you anything you want!" I screamed, "want-want-want" echoing through the universe. Security escorted me out.

In desperation I tried the direct route—prayer. People always brag that God answered their prayers or delivered a miracle. It didn't work for me in the hospital when I prayed to save Collin's life, but you never know—maybe I didn't do it right or the connection was bad since I hadn't used it before. Perhaps I dialed the wrong number.

I got down on my knees, genuflected, pressed my palms together, and lifted the receiver.

Our father, who art in heaven . . .

The line is still dead. God does not accept my calls.

Astral Email

To: God
BCC: Collin, the inveterate gamer
Re: Complaint about Life

God,

I tried to get through on the phone, but your tech support is FUBAR. If my call is so damned important, then why don't you answer?

I'm disgusted with *Life*. Your latest video game, that is. My husband and I downloaded it from Stork.net, read the manual, and got everything working. We spent years creating our heroes. We were so proud of them! We named hero one Matthew. He is dashing and strong, sensitive and caring. Hero two, Collin, we made intelligent and funny, charismatic and daring. Hero three, Katie, is musical, hardworking, compassionate, and intuitive.

All three did well for a while. Collin impressed us in the growth scenarios with how he overcame one obstacle after another—we expected him to have a terrific run. However, he hadn't even made it to the adult level when the program crashed! The explosion burned my husband and me, Matthew and Katie were damaged, and Collin was gone. Disappeared into cyberspace. Who's the idiot who left out the "save" feature?

Collin had no chance. He had no weapons cache, no bombs or missiles. You could have given him an invisibility cloak, or an awesome armored Hummer, or some Mario mushrooms, or something! And only one life? Every game on the market gives you multiple lives or replays.

I looked on the internet, but couldn't find any cheats to get Matt or Katie to the next level. They float through the screens with little engagement. I even tried to reset the game, but I can't find a reset button.

No self-respecting gamer would endorse this game. We are all your beta testers, suckers as the celestial edition of the Angel virus crashes our systems. Collin created a society on *Sim City* better than this.

Early reviews for this game were glowing. *MacWorld* gave it four mice for action & adventure and rated it R for sex and violence—a sure hit! But you only get one play and it self-destructs like a *Mission Impossible* tape.

So now we've got this empty box, this useless game. Matt and Katie are hanging in there, but I know if it crashes again, they'll be gone too. The installer made a mess—the parts are littered all over our hard drive. We can't delete them from our system. A dialogue box comes up to remind me every time I turn on the computer.

So, God. we want our hero back. Can you do data recovery? I don't suppose there's an update planned anytime soon? How about *Reincarnation: The Game?* How can you live with yourself after fucking with our lives this way? Give us hope and then snatch it away without any explanation?

Well, God, you'll probably trash this email just like all the others. At least I got to say (if some flunky angel doesn't delete this) that *Life* sucks. And I got to tell you what I think of you, up there all high and mighty, laughing at us mortals playing your unreliable, unfair, unwinnable game. As my friend Kelly says, "Seriously, God—WTF?!"

You know, one customer's bad experience can be damaging, marketing-wise. Everyone in our huge family knows about your scam. My husband and I will keep *Life* going for Matt & Katie, but we won't get suckered into any more of your games. Me, I'll stick to word processing and make-your-own greeting cards.

No reply necessary.

S.

Personal Myths

*I*f only I knew why. That search for answers has driven my grief work. Assured a good reason, it might be easier to resign myself to what happened. Perhaps, even, to accept. But despite the declarations of the religious faithful, no one has ever satisfactorily explained to me why we live and die, suffer, triumph, and mourn. It's all a big secret (although religions find this sells better when called a mystery), and there are just too many discrepancies and outright contradictions in the explanations people offer. I needed to decide: What was the nature of my faith? What happens when we die? What is the purpose of life?

My search began after Collin's death as something resembling denial. To connect with him, I sought out books about near-death experiences. Betty J. Eadie's *Embraced by the Light* and Raymond Moody's *Life After Life* promised that Collin lived on in a different form. John Edward and George Anderson, mediums who claim contact with the dead, teased me with promises that I could communicate with Collin across the ether.

I tried—tried to feel his presence, learned to meditate so I might hear his voice, tried to induce lucid dreams so I could go to him. My night visions didn't come close to recreating the lush dreamscape of the Robin Williams movie *What Dreams May Come.* Instead, I got nightmares—endless chases, fruitless searches; looping scenes in which I was stalked, stabbed, and raped. A dozen times my husband sprang awake to my bloodcurdling screams, as I saw hovering over me (in my dream? in reality?) a dark, amorphous shape sweating evil.

Perhaps I needed training, practice, to connect with Collin. I kept a dream journal as recommended by Judith Orloff in *Second Sight* and tuned in to mind-body clues for insight as described by Mona Lisa Schulz in *Awakening Intuition*. They didn't help me connect with my son.

In *Many Lives, Many Masters*, Brian L. Weiss put a human face on reincarnation and karma—something that, as a Catholic, I had never seriously considered. I learned that reincarnation was originally included in early Christian teachings, only later disavowed by the Catholic Church under Emperor Constantine in the first century C.E. at the Council of Nicaea. Wondering what else the Church had suppressed, I read about the Gnostic gospels, writings declared heretical by the Council.

The Gnostics believed the earth was created by a lesser, rather evil god called a demiurge (the Old Testament's vengeful Yahweh), who evicted Adam and Eve from the Garden of Eden after the snake told them they could access more knowledge than the god had shown them. Thus evil is a purposeful design element of life, and we work to escape it for the realm of the good, supreme God.

Intrigued more by the title than anything else, I read *God is a Verb: Kabbalah and the Practice of Mystical Judaism* by David A. Cooper. Rabbi Cooper states:

> Satan, the force of fragmentation, is the crucial element required for creation, because without it everything would unite with God—everything would become one. This does not mean that the splintering force of Satan is separate from the unity of God, but, paradoxically, that it is contained within the oneness of the Divine.

Cooper suggests we think of God as a process, a "be-ing, rather than as a thing or person."

I was surprised how much Kabbalah made sense. Stripped of modernisms like the English Mass and priestly celibacy, might Catholicism offer comfort and explanation after all? Maybe another faith might fit the bill. I began to explore, reading *The World's Living Religions* by Archie J. Bahm. Hinduism seemed prohibitively complicated, Islam too mired in ancient misogyny and modern fanaticism, and Buddhism too detached. I wanted simplicity, intelligence, and passion.

Newer faiths such as Sylvia Browne's *Novus Spiritus* and Ernest Holmes's *Science of Mind* looked promising, the former based on the Gnostic quest for knowledge and knowing oneself as the way to knowing God, the latter on the belief that God is a universal mind within us and expressed through us, with whom we must strive to become one. Both encourage asking questions and striving for knowledge of the divine and emphasize spirituality's personal nature along with the fellowship gained by connecting with others traveling a similar path. Neither elevates guilt or suffering nor demands blind faith.

From *The Ways of the Mystic: Seven Paths to God* by Joan Borysenko, I began to glean how similar most mainstream religions are. Each incorporates some version of the Golden Rule, teaches through stories, and attempts to explain natural phenomena. There are also other, more esoteric parallels: Roman Catholicism venerates seven sacraments, Kabbalah recognizes seven earthly branches of its Tree of Life, Buddha searched for seven years and rounded the Bodhi tree seven times, Hinduism states that life flows through the body in seven chakras, and Native Americans note seven directions in their Medicine Wheel.

The idea of spirituality as separate from religion began to coalesce in me. Neale Donald Walsch's *Conversations with God* presented God as personally accessible without the need for ordained intermediaries and constantly speaking to us through such mundane channels as song lyrics, the dialogue in a novel, or the wind's caress. Indeed, I often felt Collin communicated with me through songs.

In *A Woman's Journey to God*, Joan Borysenko wrote that women are spiritual by nature, and "tend to experience direct connection with the divine," seeing God "in others.... For women there really is no journey. Life and spirituality are one and the same." Walsch and Borysenko showed me that, although my religious bond has always been tenuous, I am intensely spiritual in my own way. And this spirituality has power.

Caroline Myss and Rosalyn L. Bruyere said that the power of spirit can be channeled for healing. Too late for Collin, perhaps, but the concept intrigued me. Bruyere taught me to see auras, but I never managed to sense the pulse of another person's energy enough to begin to direct it. Perhaps this ranged just a little beyond my belief zone.

Around that time, several books appeared on the market about prayer's restorative power. Although I approached with definite cynicism since my prayers for Collin's life had been ignored, I couldn't help but be impressed by the tremendous body of anecdotal and scientific evidence presented by Larry Dossey, Dale A. Matthews, and Bernie S. Siegel. People who prayed, or were prayed for, healed faster than those not prayed for. But did this have something to do with God, or were individuals tapping into some collective unconscious?

Some authors debunked near-death experiences as visions of heaven and claimed instead that these are brain events that can be recreated in the laboratory. Others jumped into the fray, discussing whether the brain activity meant heaven and God were fictions or whether stimulation of those brain areas opened a portal to the divine. Ken Wilber and Patrick Glynn examined the physiology of belief. Their books—*The Marriage of Sense and Soul: Integrating Science and Religion* and *God: The Evidence: The Reconciliation of Faith and Reason in a Postsecular World*, respectively—attest that the proclivity for faith and religion is hard-wired into humans and nurtured by the mystical events people of every culture experience.

Andrew Newberg, Eugene D'Aquili, and Vince Rause joined the debate, writing in *Why God Won't Go Away: Brain Science and the Biology of Belief*: "A neurological approach . . . suggests that God is not the product of a cognitive, deductive process, but was instead 'discovered' in a mystical or spiritual encounter made known to human consciousness through the transcendent machinery of the mind." Thus, we didn't create God—the doorway to God lies deep inside our brains.

So it seemed the concept of God revolves around consciousness. Are there different levels of consciousness, and can we on earth access them all? Is heaven a place or dimension, or a figment of our imaginations—and can we distinguish between the two? Is everything we experience a conscious fantasy?

In a fascinating look at animal consciousness, Rupert Sheldrake showed that dogs are somehow able to intuit when their owners are on their way home. He attributed this to different types of consciousness—local consciousness within individuals and non-local consciousness beyond our bodies that we tap into, similar to Jung's collective unconscious.

Jane Katra and Russell Targ also explored this theory in *The Heart of the Mind: How to Experience God Without Belief*. They offered non-local consciousness as an explanation for psychic ability, mystical transcendence, out-of-body experiences, communication with the dead, knowledge of other lives (perceived as one's own previous incarnations), and prayer's curative power. The authors quoted Albert Einstein, who invoked quantum theory. We think we are all separate beings, said Einstein, due to an "optical delusion of our consciousness" caused by not quite understanding the relationship between space and time.

In *Infinite Mind: Science of the Human Vibrations of Consciousness*, Valerie V. Hunt likens the mind to a "field" that may exist in multiple locations and interact with other fields:

> Is it possible that the long undetectable energy of the human mind springs from the electron energy of the body's atoms? Energy in this form, permeating all tissues, does not need to be conducted through the nervous system. The mind-field would then be a literal super-conductor. If the electron spin-off from the body atoms is the source of the mind's energy, then the mind might also reabsorb free electrons from the universe. Since there are no mechanical losses in such a system, the mind energy is literally recycled in the environment.

In addition to reading, I attended conferences and retreats in an attempt to connect with Collin and grok the answers to my questions. In the fall of 1998, Kelly and I attended a three-day Body & Soul spirituality conference in Boston. Our hotel was across from the Staples Center, and delivery trucks kept us awake most of the night. Then the Boston University marching band woke us at 7:30 Saturday morning with a rousing rendition of "Louie Louie."

Thankfully, the conference was wonderful, with keynotes, seminars, and hands-on exercises by leaders in the field of spirituality. Marianne Williamson offered ideas to heal America and ourselves, Neale Donald Walsch told us about talking with God, Bernie Siegel discussed the role of spirit in healing, and John O'Donohue shared the Celtic belief that the rhythms of nature and people are intertwined. Medium James Van Praagh did readings, and I was sure one of the messages was from Collin, but Van Praagh chose someone else to receive the message. Brian Weiss took us through a past-life regression, and I saw myself in a nurse's uniform and white cap with a red cross on it as I tended wounded soldiers in a battlefield tent. Barbara Brennan explained energy fields and taught us how to see auras, and we had our auras photographed. Mine was all red, which supposedly signifies excitement, leadership, and power, and I had "a deep hurt" in the heart area.

During the conference, the Robin Williams movie *What Dreams May Come* premiered. Its title comes from *Hamlet's* "To be or not to be" soliloquy: "For in that sleep of death what dreams may come." Presenters said its vision of the afterlife reflected the latest theories of experts, and the conference even set up a bus to take attendees to see it. Whether its depiction is true or not, it offered me solace to believe that Collin might be living this type of wonderful new life.

The following year, Kelly and I attended one day of Omega Institute's Healing the Whole Self conference in Fort Lauderdale. We heard Wayne Dyer suggest using the wisdom of the ages, as embodied in Pythagoras, Buddha, Jesus, Shakespeare, and Emerson, to effect deep spiritual change in ourselves and the world. Cheryl Richardson, a life coach, presented an action plan to deepen personal relationships and build a soulful community. Joan Borysenko and Candace Pert held a conversation about blending ancient cultures with new ideas.

I also attended a three-day retreat at the Omega Center in New York, where I participated in a workshop with Rosalyn Bruyere on how to sense and send energy and another on poetry writing.

I even met with a local wellness guru who taught me to meditate (this was long before meditation was a "thing") using deep breathing.

As I struggled to understand, I read more than one hundred books and attended dozens of lectures. This discourse has helped me examine the meaning of life, faith, and consciousness from different perspectives and enabled me to put together pieces of my puzzle. There are still huge gaps, and I suspect there always will be more than a few lost pieces, but I have reached a point at which I can put the puzzle back into its box. I have constructed a few scenarios that seem reasonable possibilities and realize this is as far as I can go at present.

First, I considered it possible that there is no God. This suggests that bad things happen as random events and evil is a choice people make to create their own meaning. However, the evidence I read argued against chaos theory as the universe's managing principle. I believe intuitively in a creator or director, humanlike or otherwise. Someone or something had to put evolution into motion. Plus, convinced a loving God couldn't have taken away my son, I tried out atheism. It was lonely and frightening to think life was arbitrary and meaningless and Collin just disappeared. I need to believe there is something more and anticipate an eventual reunion. (I am aware that such a choice means donning blinders not so different from those worn by people of blind faith whom I excoriate for their unwillingness to question.) Perhaps I am too cowardly or idealistic for atheism.

So, then, is God a real figure or an abstract concept? I have explored theories for each possibility.

If God is a being who created us (whether through evolution or some Biblical genesis is immaterial here), there are major questions to consider. Did God create everything and then back off to let it play out on its own, or does he or she remain involved in PTA meetings and cleaning the toilet? Is there a script, or is he not the omniscient we've been led to believe? Does she want us to follow the Golden Rule, or does she get a charge out of the continuing saga of our indiscretions and ignominies? Is there a purpose to life for us, or are we merely God's action figures (not superhero ones, surely!)?

Imagining a vindictive or careless God is horrifying (unless one embraces the Gnostic duality of an evil god and a good one). I choose to believe that if God is a real entity, he or she is good and has created a world that spins toward a larger purpose and thus does not need to interfere in day-to-day events. In many ways, this mirrors what most major religions claim.

My husband, who kindly teases me about my "Buddha books," is able to clear all thoughts from his mind. While zoning out, he has, without trying, conversed with our son. Collin told Ed there is a larger purpose that, with our limited sight, we are unable to understand. Someday, Collin said, we will see the big picture, as he now does.

Then, the conundrum: if God is good, why does he allow misery? For the logic of this paradigm to make sense, suffering must serve a purpose: teach a lesson; frame an evil lesser god's handiwork, which we must overcome to reach the good God, as the Gnostics believe; or be insignificant in the larger scheme.

If in that other consciousness we call heaven there truly is no evil, perhaps we need to learn to overcome it before we are ready for heaven. Maybe we reincarnate on earth until we stop being assholes, and then graduate to heaven. Sylvia Browne claims that, before birth, we set tasks for ourselves to accomplish on earth to enrich our souls. I could see myself, arrogant in my heavenly bliss, deciding that for my soul-lesson I could "handle" the experience of my child's death. Or, as my friend Michelle suggested, maybe I "took one for the team," agreeing to endure the unendurable to help all souls "understand the true depths of love and loss in human form."

Perhaps all the terrible things we curse God for were set in motion by the Gnostics' lesser god to let us experience ourselves as separate from God, and our struggles are our efforts to return to the good God's oneness and wholeness.

Or maybe heaven, for all its good, is boring, and life on earth is a great adventure, a Six Flags Universe amusement park. Sure, you're scared on the roller coaster, but you know it will soon end and leave you exhilarated. Souls experience the rush of life's ups and downs but know subconsciously that they will soon return to safety. Our culture abounds in risk-takers—skydivers, bungee jumpers, rock climbers, and race car drivers revel in the adrenalin of danger. Brilliant storyteller J. K. Rowling may have been prescient when she wrote in *Harry Potter and the Sorcerer's Stone*, "To the well-organized mind, death is but the next great adventure."

We humans believe the universe revolves around us even though Copernicus long ago exposed the fallacy of that egocentrism. But what if our comings and goings are too inconsequential to matter? Horrific events on earth are but blips in the cosmic eternity? A child whose toy doll breaks thinks the world is ending, but her parents know she will smile tomorrow as she hugs her stuffed dog. Collin told my husband that he will see us tomorrow—not tomorrow, our time, but tomorrow, his time. Perhaps to God we are just wailing children whose notion of time is thirty-minute intervals of *Paw Patrol* and *Sesame Street*.

Still, I wonder why such a God couldn't have come up with a better scheme. Couldn't we know in advance that our master plan comprised being robbed at gunpoint?

I think it's more probable God is not a human-like being at all, but a force comparable to gravity or electromagnetism. Many experts suggest that this force is love. Albert Einstein called God the "organizing principle of the universe." This force must then obey specific rules—the problem is, we don't yet understand the force or its rules, just as in the twelfth century lightning seemed magical. This, too, fits with Collin's assertion that we are not able to understand the big picture. Quantum physics also complicates things, yet explains how God can be everywhere at once, connected to everyone and everything, and how our participation affects events.

It solves several such problems to imagine God as the universe and all the universe a part of God (in Kabbalah it is Satan who represents the physical universe). The universe is analogous to God's body:

planets are equivalent to bones; space, God's circulatory system. Stars are brain neurons firing, and light is the emanation of God's thoughts. Plant and animal networks on earth act as organ systems that maintain the body's balance. Carnivores are white blood cells, gobbling invaders. Scavengers are the excretory system, recycling used material.

What place do humans occupy in this organic machine? Viruses, perhaps, multiplying exponentially and intent on destroying our host. Or cells, the evil ones gone awry as cancers. Or, my favorite: perhaps we are sense organs—God's senses.

If God is a spiritual, bodiless being or force, then God cannot directly experience sensation. But if God's body is the universe, God has sense organs—us. We feel everything, good and bad, thrill and pain. This would explain the awful things that happen to us—and God's indifference. Every day, we humans burn nerve endings in our tongues with hot coffee, destroy hearing cells with leaf blowers and stereos—and we don't mourn these cells' deaths. Similarly, if we are the cells that enable God to see and feel and smell, God does not agonize over our anguish. We are all connected, parts of a living machine that needs every element to function. When cells in our bodies die, they are excreted back to the earth or recycled within the body to make new cells. When we die, our energy is likewise reclaimed into God's body in a different form for another purpose. "For life and death are one, even as the river and the sea are one," wrote visionary poet Kahlil Gibran.

In a similar manner, my old faith has been reabsorbed and recast. Collin's death destroyed the faith I thought I had. If psychologist and philosopher Joseph Campbell is correct that the need for such beliefs is hardwired into deep-brain structures, I have no choice. I *must* create a new guiding explanation—a myth, in the classic sense—for myself. It is not necessary for me to embrace one definitive theory. Multiple possibilities are perhaps more intriguing and invite further thought. In fact, I don't even have to actively construct one. Campbell said, "You don't create myths. Myths come like dreams. You have to wait for them. . . . Each of us must recognize and make explicit the myths that do come, and the myths we live by. For we all live by a myth of some kind." These, then, are my current myths about life and death, suffering and evil, and God.

What are yours?

VIII
A Family Shattered

*Death is a dispassionate AR-15—
aiming to hit one luckless target,
it sprays everyone nearby.*

This book is about my experience of grief, so originally I included little about Ed or Matt and Katie. Early readers of the manuscript, however, suggested that my family's struggles informed mine and thus were integral context. I agree. So I've sprinkled details of their grief stories throughout and added sections in this chapter in their own words.

Theseus Unarmed

*E*ventually, we all grieve. Some mourn the loss of innocence or youth, others a lost job or squandered opportunity. Many will feel, at best, at loose ends as a relationship unravels; at worst, terror at slipping through a swiftly-swelling hole. And few escape despair's stranglehold after the death of a beloved.

Grief is a universal human experience like birth, eating, sex, love, death. And yet grief is also a most local experience—more personal than sex, more misunderstood than love. Selfish, cloistered, it is the one human experience that resists sharing. "A whisper in the world and a clamor within," former *New York Times* columnist Anna Quindlen called it.

In other life circumstances, the clamor is shared. Experienced mothers help expectant ones prepare for baby's arrival, and we eagerly await the joyful recounting of vital statistics and declare the new name perfect. Eating is such a collective endeavor that we congregate not only with family or friends for meals in our homes, but with strangers at restaurants. Strategies for mind-blowing sex ooze from the TV and internet; advice about love is proffered by BFFs.

The tender conversation of a deathbed vigil is a poignant gift to both the dying one and the survivor, and an entire industry has grown around helping with funeral arrangements. But even though we are all experienced mourners, we stand speechless before the bereaved, or say the wrong things, or have no clue how to comfort. And so we slink away, our lack of communion compounding the griever's loss and leaving him, as Theseus, to meet the Minotaur alone and unarmed.

In *Becoming*, Michelle Obama wrote about the loneliness of grief:

It hurts to live after someone has died. It just does. It can hurt to walk down a hallway or open the fridge. It hurts to put on a pair of socks, to brush your teeth. Food tastes like nothing. Colors go flat. Music hurts, and so do memories. You look at something you'd otherwise find beautiful—a purple sky at sunset or a playground full of kids—and it only somehow deepens the loss. Grief is so lonely this way.

It is not our own selfishness that holds us back, but grief's. As individual as a fingerprint, there is no one-size-fits-all. Even two people who experience the same loss, such as parents of a child, will experience it in different ways.

My friend Lynne drank when she heard her dead son's footsteps on the stairs. Aunt Sal became a recluse and insisted she died the night her husband was murdered. Mom's friend Ginny focused on her faith when her empty home echoed with questions. My sister, Collin's godmother, became depressed and left her freewheeling singles life in Fort Lauderdale to move in with us. My mother coped with the death of her grandson by becoming a worker ant; my father by donning a coat of igneous rock.

I read. And wrote. And slept. And talked and cried and screamed. I wore my grief on the outside. But my husband and kids kept theirs to themselves. Matt stopped going to class and flunked out of college. I found Katie throwing up in the bathroom in the middle of the night. She had tried to drink herself to death. My husband went right back to work, keeping us afloat financially since I couldn't. He swallowed his grief, chewing it into a cancer that bit back.

Ed's Story

I adore my kids. In the backyard, I taught them all to hit and field. I helped coach their Little League teams—even Katie played Tee Ball. We took a lot of family day trips to places like Fort Delaware, a Civil War prison, and the Smithsonian Museum in Washington, D. C. The boys worked with me as painters during the summers, and Katie waited anxiously to be old enough to join the fun. When Collin died, I was devastated.

Just before the accident, I was playing basketball in our driveway with Collin and Katie and Collin's friend Patrick. Collin shouldn't have been there at all. He skipped his first school baseball game when his uniform didn't fit. Unperturbed, Collin seemed satisfied that the coach would work it out before the next game. We had a blast, and he seemed particularly happy to laugh and tease with his friend on such a glorious day.

Susan was conducting a computer workshop at school, so when the game broke up, I went inside to fix spaghetti for dinner. Suddenly, Katie ran into the kitchen screaming for me.

I rushed outside to find Collin lying motionless in the street, his eyes glassy, foam bubbling between his lips, neon red streaming from his nose and ear. I ran to call 911. When I came back outside, Katie was holding Collin's head still, blood soaking her jeans. I sent Katie's best friend, Stefania, into the house to call Susan. I could hear her trying to explain what had happened.

"Tell her to come NOW!" I yelled, my voice a growl. "It's really bad!"

The ambulance arrived quickly, and the attendants loaded Collin into the truck. I followed. Instead of pulling out onto the main road from our neighborhood, the ambulance stopped at the red light for about twenty minutes. Collin had become combative, something we later learned is common in people with head injuries.

Finally we arrived, and the attendants wheeled Collin into the ER. Someone took me to a small closet of a room where Susan was waiting. Later, our cousin Lynn told us that hospital staff called this the "crying room." You know, on TV, someone with a head injury barely touches down in the ER before being raced up to the OR. But this was real life, in slow motion. It seemed a half hour before the neurosurgeon arrived, another forty-five minutes before he talked to us, and yet another forty-five before Collin was finally taken into surgery.

After several hours, we finally got to see our son. Susan and I clung to each other in the hallway, crying. This was my first inkling that Collin might not pull through, but in my shock, I believed that, of course, he would be okay.

I was overcome with guilt. If I hadn't gone inside to cook dinner, Collin might be at home in his own bed, safely asleep right now.

Next came the longest five days of my life, although I couldn't tell you much about what happened except for sitting at Collin's bedside and praying in the chapel a couple of times. When the nurses kicked us out of Collin's room, I just zoned out in front of the TV or let our friends and family distract me. It hadn't hit me that Collin might die. That Monday, the neurosurgeon said they would bring Collin out of his coma over several days. We weren't sure whether he would wake up or what shape he would be in, but I had renewed hope that he would survive. I left the hospital to take Katie to school. Susan called us back in, and I was scared the worst was going to happen. Then Susan said Collin was gone, and the doctors confirmed that he was brain-dead. I was angry—I thought things had turned around. I wasn't ready for it to happen yet.

I know in my head that organ donation helps many people. But the whole process left a bad taste in my mouth. The interview to determine which body parts we would donate was hellish. Then, as soon as we agreed to donate Collin's organs, the staff descended in the blink of an eye, like vultures. I knew they had to do tests for the transplants and every second counts, but it just seemed so cold. Our son had died, and no one took our feelings into account.

The next days were a blur as we planned Collin's funeral. The sight of a roomful of sample caskets at the funeral home jolted me from my daze. It was like seeing my worst nightmare. Susan and her dad kept me from falling. Then one day I woke up and Collin was just gone, forever.

Susan was a mess. She was up all night crying, then slept all day. She could barely hold a coherent conversation. It was up to me to keep our family afloat financially. As an independent contractor, if I didn't work, I didn't get paid. E. Robinson Painting didn't care that my son was dead. I pushed my grief down into a hole—buried it like my son—and went back to work. I understand how women who are beaten or raped block everything out and don't remember. You just put the pain in a box and don't think about it.

We needed the money I brought in. But it was also good for me to go back to work. Sitting home all day marinating in my grief would have been excruciating. Susan's thoughts ran marathons in her head (Dr. W. called them intrusive thoughts), but my way of dealing with trauma was to zone out, almost to turn off my thoughts. The physical work of painting distracted me from pain and provided an outlet for my anxiety.

Plus, for me, work was more than a way to make money. President-elect Biden said his dad had always told him that a job was about more than just work. The same was true for me. I had worked hard to grow my business and loved my job, loved interacting with homeowners, many of whose children I'd watched grow up and have their own babies. It gave me a sense of purpose, accomplishment, and self-respect. I don't know who I'd have become without it.

With Susan not teaching, our income was cut nearly in half. I felt that burden every day. If I collapsed, our family would collapse, and it would be my fault. We managed until the 2008 financial crisis, when work slowed and income dropped off. I needed to lay off Matt, but he had a new house with a hefty mortgage. It was either let Matt lose his house or get myself into trouble with the IRS. I stopped paying payroll taxes. A year later, when I finally admitted to Susan the financial trouble we were in, we owed thousands, plus interest and penalties.

The anxiety and depression that had been hiding around every corner finally jumped out and bit me. Rather than sadness, it came out as anger. Never before in my life a mean person, I snapped at everyone. I lashed out at people who made Susan cry, the pile of bills on the kitchen table, and drivers on the road. Susan convinced me to seek treatment, and it helped.

Still, tamping down my grief 24/7, while working and taking care of my family and our household, was exhausting. I painted all day, then cooked dinner and escaped to my recliner and the drone of the TV. An audiophile and former music major, I loved music, especially classical pieces. But after Collin died, I lost all interest. Listening for the nuances in the music felt like too much trouble, required too much focus.

What I did focus on was trying to fix things for Susan and the kids. It felt like my responsibility to get my family back again. But when I tried to comfort Susan, she pushed me away. Everything I did seemed to put additional pressure on her and make things worse. I felt like I was failing her. At the same time, my feelings were hurt because I needed her comfort, needed to be close to her, to have her hug me and say things would be okay. Consumed by her own grief, she had nothing to give. And she wanted me to talk about my feelings, which I was trying my best to suppress.

I found less invasive ways to look out for Susan and protect her feelings. I bought her stars to remind her of Collin. Told her she was the sexiest woman in the world when she fretted over gaining weight. Took over cooking dinner and helped out with other household chores she couldn't deal with. Took the kids to lunch and talked to them. One year I decorated the Christmas tree all by myself, then put everything away afterward.

Unable to help, unable to be helped, we lived as roommates for several years. We never fought, but there was no intimacy, sexual or emotional. I realized that was just the way it was going to be, and I loved her so much it didn't make any difference. We could easily have separated, as many bereaved parents do, but our love and respect for each other, along with our love for our children, sustained us as we waited out the storm. Time helped us find our way back together and we became lovers again. Now we think of ourselves as "beyond love," so close we're almost like one person.

Today, I still keep my grief under wraps. It has become a way of life to hunker down, press through, and close everything out. But like a leaky faucet, it drips out here and there when something triggers it. I break down a lot at the cemetery and sometimes when I'm driving alone in my truck.

I cried for days after my Australian Shepherd, Finn, died. The happiest dog, Finn never had a bad day until he got cancer, a grapefruit-sized ball on his shoulder. When he lost his zest for life and struggled with pain, we had the vet euthanize him. I felt like I killed my buddy.

My grief roared out big time when we dealt with the organ donation organization. I felt Collin had been hoodwinked and betrayed when, a year after he died, none of his organ recipients had bothered to thank him for the gift of life. We met with officials to suggest ways recipients could be encouraged to send thank you cards to donor families, but the powers that be decided it would be too upsetting— people have a hard time adjusting, they told us. Yeah, we had a hard time adjusting to our son's death. We'd have fallen all over ourselves to thank those who gave him new life. Eventually, we were gratified to receive heartfelt letters from the recipients of Collin's heart and kidney.

One time grief totally disabled me. When my sister-in-law was pregnant with her daughter, we moved Collin's things into another bedroom and converted his room into a nursery. Susan asked me to paint one wall in the new room. I put it off and put it off, then finally just told her I couldn't do it. I just couldn't deal with it. I wasn't ready to face the grief and pain.

Swallowing my grief, holding it deep down in my gut, came at a cost. It devoured me from the inside out. Just before 9/11, I felt physically tired and weak all the time, unable to sweep a sidewalk or wash the car. Susan made me see the doctor, and we learned I had colon cancer. Two weeks later I had surgery, which left a long scar down my belly. They got it all, so no radiation or chemo was needed. A week later I was back in the hospital because my incision was infected. That stay lasted another week. I came home for a couple days, then ended up in the hospital a third time with severe abdominal pain. Test after test came back negative. Finally the surgeon said he needed to open me up and see what was going on. My gall bladder was gangrenous. Another long scar, another week in the hospital. Two weeks later I was back at work.

For the past several years, I've dealt with one health issue after another—heart disease, an irregular heartbeat, high cholesterol and blood pressure. Bursitis in my shoulder made painting a struggle. Then I had severe knee and leg pain, which doctors say is due to a bulging lumbar disc. Most recently, I had a stroke in my spinal column and experience frequent nausea, dizziness, shortness of breath, and stiffness in my jaw. I still don't have a diagnosis for these. Susan wonders if the symptoms are my body's way of rejecting the grief it has had to carry for more than two decades.

When I feel really low, Collin comes to give me a pep talk. He seems to know when I need him. I'll be sitting at a red light, zoning out, turning off my thoughts, when Collin tells me things will be okay—and they are. I don't hear his voice—it's more like telepathy, connecting brain to brain. I know it's not just my imagination because he talks about things I'd never think of on my own.

Collin told me he is happy and that it is wonderful where he is. He couldn't wait to go but hung around at the hospital for us because we were so devastated. However, he would no longer have been himself and didn't want to burden us with that. So after Susan told him he could go, he flew. "Don't be sad," he said, "because I'll see you tomorrow—tomorrow *my* time, not your time." An entire lifetime was like an instant to him.

I also "saw" Collin in church when we went to hear my mother-in-law's choir do their Christmas cantata. It wasn't a visual image, more a knowing that he was there, perched on the altar rail, smiling.

I miss Collin every day. It sounds crazy, but I miss the arguing, especially about baseball games. He was ornery like me and got in trouble a lot, so he delighted in sticking in the knife and turning it when Matt got caught hiding beer under a bush or the police brought Katie home in the middle of the night. When he started breaking out of his TS, people began to relate to him more. Playing basketball that beautiful March day, he was excited to be a normal kid having fun with his new friend.

I asked Collin why he had to die. He wouldn't tell me but said I'd find out someday when it was my time.

Matt's Story

*K*atie paged me 911 when I was on my way home from coaching a baseball game for Newark High School. It was my first coaching job, a JV game against Concord. The police had our street blocked off and I couldn't get to the house, so I drove to the hospital. It didn't seem real, what was happening. At first, I didn't think it could be that bad—I thought Collin would wake up. Everybody was scared though, so it seemed like it was pretty serious. It still felt like it wasn't really happening.

The week in the hospital was a blur. I hated seeing him hooked up to all those machines like he wasn't even there. Bloated and swollen, he didn't even look like my brother. Some of my friends came to stay with me, and mostly we just sat in the family waiting room. Sometimes we watched TV. No one had cell phones then, so there was nothing to do. That was fine because I just wanted to sit and think about nothing.

The day Collin died, Katie and I were supposed to go to school, but we didn't get up. Dad was mad. I know he was upset and frustrated. He came home to take Katie to school, but then we got the call from Mom to come to the hospital. I don't remember the rest of that day at all.

I had been to viewings before, but it's totally different when it's for someone you grew up with and shared so much with. It still all felt like a dream—this couldn't really be happening. I kept waiting for Collin to sit up and laugh his huge laugh and tease us about the prank he pulled on us. The boy in the casket didn't even look like my brother. He was in a plastic bag to keep anything from leaking out. He had on a hat that didn't fit him right because his head was all messed up. I didn't like it, and I don't remember him that way. My memory of Collin is the picture with Grammy and Grandfather at the University of Tennessee.

The night went on forever, waves of people moving through the line to give us a word or two of comfort and sympathy. I had to take breaks from standing with my parents next to the casket. A few times I slipped out to smoke cigarettes. My friends—Shawn, Brian, Wayne, Josh, Jordan, and Brad, all came and kept me company. Mike and Ray, two of the owners from the gas station/convenience store where I used to work, paid their respects. All through the evening, I heard the songs on the playlist I had made, and they took me back to times Collin and I spent together.

I don't remember the funeral, other than random bits and pieces, flashes almost—a song, a Collin story, tears.

At home in the weeks and months after the funeral, it felt like something was missing. Of course, Collin was missing. But the life I knew was gone too. My family collapsed around me.

Besides losing my brother, I also felt like I lost my mom. She was never the same afterward. Everything changed. We all changed, and the whole world changed for us. But Mom changed the most. Before, our house was always organized, the clutter gone every week. She held us to high standards, and if we strayed from the straight and narrow, we got the infamous "path speech" about making the right choices to stay on the path to happiness and success. She organized lots of activities that we did together as a family—parties, trips, museums. And Mom and I were close. I spent hours sitting on the kitchen counter pouring out my heart and getting her advice.

After Collin died, never again. Things didn't seem to matter to Mom anymore. The house was a mess, clutter piling up because no one straightened up. House rules disappeared. Mom was afraid Katie and I might rebel or be angry with her, so she let us do whatever we wanted. It was a good thing Mom and Dad's early parenting had been solid, and it helped that I was an adult, more equipped to handle the changes. There were no more family events or outings. We all just lived in our own little bubbles. I couldn't add to Mom's burdens, so there were no more kitchen counter talks. I was never mad or hurt about how things were. I never felt abandoned. It was just weird how all the things we used to do suddenly didn't happen anymore.

Mom was "gone" for a long time—years. It's only in the last several years that she seems to have come out of the fog. When I had my own kids, I understood.

To be honest, Mom and I might have drifted apart even if Collin hadn't died, but a perfect storm of factors made it more sudden and more obvious. I was living in the basement and going to college, and I had been raised to be independent. When I wasn't in class, I hung out with my friends or was out somewhere. We just lived separate lives.

Even before Collin died, I wasn't sure I wanted to be in college. I didn't know what I wanted to do with my life. It didn't help that I wasn't accepted to the University of Delaware's main campus and had to do the parallel program. That felt just like high school—not very exciting. After Collin died, I had an extra excuse to quit doing what I didn't want to do anyway. So I stopped going to school and failed out. I appealed, explaining that my brother died and I was depressed, and they reinstated me. The dean in the parallel program told me to get over my brother's death. I could have punched her in the face. Then I promptly failed out again the next semester. You can't succeed in college if you don't go to class.

I never blamed it on Collin. I wish someone had given me more direction about where to go and helped me figure out what I wanted to do. I should have gone to Wilmington University and taken classes at 5:30 p.m. instead of sleeping through 8 a.m. classes. I could have played baseball for WilmU instead of saddling myself with $50,000 of school debt. But I have no regrets. I made a good life, have two great kids. Maybe I wouldn't have those kids if I had gone a different route.

After Collin died, I became less interested in friendships. I didn't want to be around people—I just wanted to sit and not be bothered. I had always been friends with lots of different people, but I drew back from all but my best friends. They hung out with me in my room, but we were nineteen, twenty, and sometimes they wanted to party. I didn't want to do that.

Dad had a lot of stress on his shoulders. Everything weighed on him immensely. He was carrying Mom and us, but no one was carrying him. Still, he never took it out on us. I always looked up to that as the way I'd need to be. I still try to follow his example—put your head down and work. Sometimes people ask me how I work three jobs, weekends. I tell them I have to do it so I just do it.

Dad didn't let me sit around and mope. If you're not going to college, he said, you have to do something. He offered to teach me the painting business. It seemed like a good thing to do, more to spend time with Dad than because I wanted to paint. It was a decent job, and I was able to buy a house and a nice car. I never thought I'd go back to college after that—thought that would be it for me. But I did go back and got my degree plus two master's and became a teacher and now an administrator.

Collin and I were close growing up, and I never really understood that there was anything wrong with him. I remember a time when we were little, maybe five and three. We were riding in the car down Mendenhall Mill Road, and he and I snickered back and forth about Santa, smiled, and laughed. It was a happy time. We had just moved into a new house, and everything was good. I knew he had to take medicine every day and had these pill carriers with the days of the week on them. Mom and Dad took him to see Dr. W. all the time, and he was in the hospital once. Maybe because I was young then I didn't understand. His behavior never seemed like a problem for me until he got older and was always getting into trouble. Then it was weird.

At one point, Mom and Dad thought he might have ADHD and made him cut down on sugar. When we went with Mom to the grocery store, we were each allowed to pick out a cereal. Collin wasn't allowed to pick one that had sugar as the first ingredient. He had a fit. Of course you want to stick it to your brother, so I was delighted.

Katie and I weren't as close as Collin and I because she was so much younger and a girl. Even today, we don't hang out together. Especially after Collin died, with Dad working all the time and Mom AWOL, I felt like a parent to Katie, felt like I had to protect her.

Losing Collin bothers me more now than it did right after he died. I see all these guys doing fun things with their brothers, and Collin and I should have that too. I only got to have him through adolescence, and by then we were fighting. I thought his childhood was stolen, and then he was taken. He was always behind, developmentally, then he finally started to get better and we became friends again and—fuck! He didn't get to experience what the rest of us did. My brother wasn't at my wedding. We didn't get to go out for a beer together. He didn't get to meet my kids, and it sucks that he's not here to raise our kids together. I wish I could see the man he'd have become.

Katie's Story

*I*t was a really nice day, a taste of spring. We were all out playing basketball—me, Dad, Collin, Pat. It was one of the best times I'd ever had with Collin. He wasn't his normal pain-in-the-ass self. Dad called it to start dinner. Collin and Pat walked to Pat's car parked across the street and started messing around. I rolled my eyes—*those two idiots.* "I'm going down to Stefania's," I said.

I passed Dad's truck and saw Pat's car move. Collin was on the hood. *Ugh. Idiots!* I thought again. I continued walking, then heard Pat slam on his brakes, heard the Sprite slosh onto the pavement. *Ugh, of course he fell.* Then it was quiet—too quiet. I looked back and saw Collin on the ground. He wasn't moving as I walked back toward him. Pat was out of the car and looked spooked. As I got closer, I could see a huge pool of blood on the ground.

I ran inside to get Dad. He was at the stove cooking spaghetti. I couldn't speak, couldn't get a word out. I just grabbed him and dragged him outside with me. He took one look and ran back inside to call 911. Pat was kneeling beside Collin. I ran across the street and sat down and held Collin's head to steady his neck because we didn't know what was wrong with him. I talked to him to try to get him to open his eyes or wake up, but he was just twitching. There was an extreme amount of blood. My jeans soaked through from my hip to my ankle. Blood was all over my hands and the front of my shirt.

Stefania came up while I sat with Collin. Dad sent her inside to call Mom. I'm not sure how long it was before the ambulance showed up. It was one of those moments when time didn't exist—in one sense it felt like just a few minutes, but at the same time it felt like forever before the paramedics and ambulance screamed to the curb.

We backed away and let them take over. Collin started physically fighting, throwing punches, struggling, but wasn't awake or aware—it was like he was drunk. They struggled for a long time to restrain him and get him into the ambulance.

Then I had my run-in with the police officer. The cop decided she needed to talk to me right then and there. She asked a million questions—his name, which I could hardly get out, and his birthday. In shock, I couldn't even talk to her. She yelled at me: "You don't even remember your own brother's birthday?" She was up in my face and grilled me as if investigating a murder.

Finally, Pat's sister, Leah, arrived and took me into the house. She made me dinner and sat with me in the kitchen, taking care of me as we waited for news from the hospital. I kept paging my brother, Matt—none of us had cell phones then. He finally turned up, and I ran to meet him a few houses down the street, as they had roped it off in front of our house. He told me to go back into the house and he took off.

While I sat with Leah in the kitchen, the officer came to the door. She was short with us and said she needed me to find out if any of our neighbors had seen anything. I was covered in my brother's blood, but she wanted me to do detective work for her. I went to a few houses, but nobody saw anything.

Finally, somebody called from the hospital and told me I needed to come. Leah couldn't take me—she needed to stay with her brother and mother, who were still in the police car at the top of our street. I was grateful she had been there for me. I don't remember who drove me to the hospital. Matt met me at the ER and walked me back to the little room with my parents. I operated like a robot, no emotion, my clothes painted in blood, just doing what I had to do.

We moved upstairs to a large waiting room. Once again, the officer tried to talk to me about the accident, but just then the surgeon came in. My cousin Bobby, a state trooper, finally sent the cop away.

That night, we passed out in a small, private waiting room and slept on some chairs we pulled together. The next morning everyone was there—family, friends. Seeing Collin was a surreal experience. He didn't look like himself. His head was all wrapped up, and he smelled weird—that chemical hospital smell. A sign above him noted that he had a skull flap on the left side.

We spent every day of spring break in the hospital. It blurred into one long day that never ended. I didn't know when one day ended or the next started. I kind of shut down, like I didn't have any feelings. I don't remember what I did. I just existed. One of the nurses tried to talk to all of us kids about the accident. I was in no mood for her to talk to me like a child. I did start drinking coffee, though. The days were long and stressful, and when we weren't sitting with Collin, we wandered to a coffee machine.

That last day, I was at home with Matt because Mom and Dad had told me I had to go back to school. I was mad, so Dad was going to pick me up and drive me. But then, instead of making the turn to go to school, he just kept driving. It took me a while to figure out where we were going.

I don't remember walking into the hospital or getting to Collin's room. Magically, I was there. Someone sat us in a little alcove off the NCCU and said, this is how it's going to work. We got to say goodbye one last time. I told my brother I loved him, squeezed his hand, and gave him a kiss. It was weird, like he wasn't there, even though his body lay in the bed. Matt and I left the room together. I was fried.

When we got home, we discovered that the church ladies had cleaned up. They got every drop of blood out of my jeans and shirt and left them neatly folded in my room. I'm still mad about that. I wasn't ready to let go.

I had nothing suitable to wear to the funeral services, so Aunt Marybeth took me shopping. She was kind and patient, trooping through multiple stores to help me find a nice dress and shoes.

Collin's viewing was a marathon. It was overwhelming—so many people, everybody saying, "I'm so sorry." I got tired of hearing it, tired of talking to people and had to take a couple of breaks. I got through on autopilot. When I touched Collin in the casket, he felt the same as he had in the hospital. It freaked me out a bit.

I didn't cry during the funeral service. I just stared straight ahead. I don't know if I took in anything that was said or that happened. I could see it all, but I just stared. When I looked out the window of the limo as everyone filed out of church, I saw my friends hanging out, talking and chatting with each other. I was angry about that.

It was pouring when we got to the cemetery. We snuggled in under the canopy as best we could. Matt grabbed my hand and I started crying, tears just rushing out of my eyes. It didn't feel like I knew I was crying, but the tears were flowing.

Back at our house, people were stacked wall to wall. I wanted everybody to leave. I didn't want anyone around. Didn't want to talk to anybody, see anybody.

I was angry but didn't know why. When I went back to school, I started having trouble with friends. I had been one of the popular girls, and my parents called me their "wild child." That flipped overnight. I wasn't twelve anymore, wasn't interested in hanging out and chattering and gossiping. My friends got tired of me, and some took it personally and made up mean things about me or told people, oh my god, don't hang out with that girl. My core group of friends stuck by me, but things were different, even with them. I just wasn't interested in doing the silly, twelve-year-old things they were excited about.

The rest of my seventh-grade year and summer are a blur. I didn't want to feel anything. In eighth grade I started having flashbacks of the accident. The first time it happened was in social studies class. We were watching a movie, and I could see the movie, could see the room, but could also see and hear and smell everything that happened *that* day. I clenched my hands so hard my nails left marks in my palms. My teachers and the school nurse were kind and understanding, but I soon started going off the rails, having flashbacks all the time at the most random, inopportune moments. It started to eat away at me. Stefania stood by me, but everyone else started to look at me like I was weird. I wanted to stop feeling the anger and sadness and pain. I snuck downstairs and drank at night so I didn't have to feel anything.

I couldn't talk to Mom and Dad because they were drowning in their own pain. I didn't want to add to their burden. I was so deep in my own shit I didn't even notice Mom wasn't hovering. I would probably have pushed her away anyway. I didn't want anyone there.

After she found me vomiting vodka in the middle of the night, Mom took me to see a psychiatrist. He was arrogant and didn't relate to me at all. He even got the story all wrong—something about Collin on a bicycle? I didn't bother to correct him. When he prescribed antidepressants, Mom said she had read that some of these caused suicidal thoughts in teens. "That's a myth," he said. He was wrong.

Then by accident, Mom found me a therapist who saved my life. Mom chaperoned a school field trip, and on the bus, another parent offered condolences and asked how I was doing. It turned out he was a psychologist, and he offered to see me. I didn't want to talk to anyone, but I talked to Dr. Z. He helped me sort through everything—the flashbacks, my friend stuff. He helped me see that I didn't need to have a million friends, and that this would eventually pass. I don't remember any of our sessions. I just remember the feeling of relief, of an enormous weight lifted. I stopped being so angry and survived middle school with a couple of friends who are still my good friends today.

High school was a lot better, as I was more comfortable with who I was. Although still friends with my best friends, I wasn't as much a one-group person. Plus, my friendship with Sonia solidified. We knew each other in seventh grade, became friends in eighth, and were good friends by freshman year. Eventually, she became my maid of honor. Sonia's dad died a couple of months before Collin. She and I were in the same classes and both took school seriously. We had the same outlook on life, having grown up overnight. We became the moms of our group, never going to parties to get trashed or high. I had already done all that in middle school.

Collin's death affected every area of my life. I had taken private flute lessons since fifth grade. Playing the flute was something I was good at and did well with. My teacher had dyslexia like I did, so she knew how to present concepts in a way that stuck with me. She had me enter a competition to be nationally ranked, in which I had to do music theory, sight read, play a prepared piece, and compose an original piece of music. My parents even bought me a new, professional flute.

It was a lot of work. I practiced two hours a day, did an hour of breath work, then worked on reading and writing music activities. But I liked it and it made me happy. After Collin died, I didn't want to do the work anymore. I didn't want to do anything anymore. My work ethic suffered and my confidence disappeared. I persevered with private lessons, but struggled with performances. My middle school band teacher pushed all of us to try out for All-State Band. I had the talent to make it but wasn't at my best on audition day. It's hard to be at your best when you question everything.

My flute teacher tried to push me back into my groove by giving me a very difficult piece. I thought I handled it well until she paired me with an accompanist who was just mean. When I had trouble coming in after the piano introduction, she hammered at me: "You should get this. Why aren't you getting this?" She didn't say it nicely, either. She had a tone. Once, I might have risen to the occasion, but I was already having trouble believing in myself. I performed the piece, but the experience put a bad taste in my mouth and made me lose confidence in my playing in general. I did less and less, and then with harder high school work and AP classes, I stopped playing altogether. If I wasn't going to be good, I thought I might as well put my time elsewhere.

Today I still have flashbacks, mostly at night, though they are few and far between. I still see it, feel it, smell it. It still feels like it happened yesterday. Not a dream, I'm fully awake and remember every detail. My husband, Joe, takes the brunt of it, sitting with me until the terror passes. He has been my rock since we started dating in high school. He came into the picture and I greeted him not with baggage, but with a whole set of luggage. Collin's death is always there with me, and Joe has to deal with the fallout. I worry sometimes whether it's too much for him, for our relationship.

My two daughters ask so many questions about Collin. Abby doesn't understand why he would do something so obviously reckless and stupid. Trying to explain that is difficult. I wish she could have met Collin. Abby has TS too, and he could have helped and mentored her. It would be heartening for her to see him as a successful, functioning adult.

It's hard to tell new people about Collin because of their reaction. New friends like my daughters' friends' moms ask about my family, then look at me with wide eyes—oh shit, sorry I asked. So mostly, I keep it to myself.

Like that Kenny Chesney song, I often wonder who Collin would be today. I also wonder who I'd be. I don't think I would be the same person. Even if I had met Joe, I doubt we would have dated or gotten married because I would still have been that "I'm popular. I have a million friends" girl. Without that push to grow up and take life seriously, I don't think I would have followed that same path.

I think about Pat a lot. His family moved away, and at one point I thought about trying to find him but didn't know whether that would make things worse for him. I just think he deserves someone to tell him it wasn't his fault. I'm the only one who saw the accident, so I'm the one who should reassure him it was Collin's decision to jump on the car.

Dark Night

I sit alone in the dark on Collin's bed, so far removed from Buddhist mindfulness it's like being in my own sensory deprivation chamber. I hear nothing of the house creaking, my family talking downstairs, the dog lying beside me on the floor. I don't know how long I've been here. Pain's clamor blocks sensory input. Or perhaps I am trying to will myself to that other dimension, the one where senses are artifacts of a dimly remembered past. My mind hiccups from thought to thought.

I do not know how I can continue to endure this pain—worse than childbirth, worse than the kidney stones doctors blasted a few years ago. The torment is physical and mental and emotional and spiritual, encompassing everything I am. My chest and head are poised to implode and explode simultaneously. My blood has surely been drained and my veins filled with liquid lead—embalmed alive. Some things I knew for sure, like my purpose in life and the love of God, have been acid-etched from my brain, leaving scorched circuits in useless gray pudding. Despair takes me past the point from which I can return, into the dark night of my own soul. There is no future there.

My son is dead. I am dead. The life pieces I painstakingly connected for forty-three years have been sundered like a giant jigsaw puzzle cruelly dashed to the floor. It's not even possible to start over, since critical pieces are missing now or crushed beyond recognition. What's next? Do I live another fifty years trying to distract myself from the pain? Do I pretend everything is fine? Turn to drugs or go on a never-ending bender? Shall I stay inside this chamber forever?

I've never been one to give up. Nothing is impossible, I used to tell my students. But I was wrong. This is impossible. There is no detour around it, no idea that will bring Collin back and restore my life. I know, because I've spent months trying to outwit death—trying to suss out one secret maneuver no one else has deduced, the loophole left for a keen and motivated mind to reverse time and set things right.

What's wrong with giving up, after all? Perhaps it's more pathetic to hold on to what will never be. A broken teacup, recemented, may be stronger than before but forever wears the tattoo of its torture. And what have all my impossible standards done for me? Collin won't return just because I never give up. As it is, my fingernails hold me to this life. The rest of me hangs, heavy—ambivalent about whether to drop down or climb up. Giving up will stop the pain. I could retreat into myself, into dreams, into fantasy, whole again. After all, who says this life is the real one? Maybe there are parallel existences devoid of grief and death. Perhaps, as Edgar Allan Poe suggested, the line between life and death is "shadowy and vague."[26] Or maybe it is not madness that is the ticket to ride, but forever-sleep.

Death. Suicide. There—I've acknowledged the demon that has dogged me for weeks now, shadowing my every move, waiting for the right moment to offer its poisoned apple. As I invite it into my chamber, I see it isn't so imposing up close. The perfect fruit has been polished to a bright sheen with not a hint of a bruise. It offers the ecstasy of oblivion, the slate's erasure. We all meet death. I'd get to choose mine. Should anyone elect to live this way?

I want the apple. One by one I perceive my senses again. My flesh tingles with anticipation. The desire becomes a sweet-sour taste in my mouth. I lick my lips and suck in a deep breath, revived. It would be easy, wouldn't it? People do it all the time. Drive my car off a bridge— I've imagined that often enough. Pick my target, close my eyes, and step on it.

Of course, there's always the chance I wouldn't die, but only get tangled in a guardrail and just be maimed—or hurt someone else. There aren't any good open cliffs in Delaware and I'm not going to drive around for hours searching for a spot.

---

[26] "The boundaries which divide Life from Death are at best shadowy and vague. Who shall say where the one ends, and where the other begins?" —Edgar Allan Poe

Carbon monoxide? Just go to sleep. But it turns your skin a funny color. That couldn't be my children's last vision of me.

A gun then. No—not my style. I've hated guns since Uncle Bob was murdered. Besides, I don't have the energy to go buy one. Turning over in bed is a chore that requires planning.

This is harder than I thought.

Pills—the unequivocal choice of women, I guess. But would my medicine cabinet's combination of Tylenol, Nyquil, and antidepressants do the job? How would I know I've taken enough to do more than ravage my gut? Besides, I've always suspected some women take pills to allow time for someone to swoop in just ahead of the grim reaper and rescue them.

A romantic (if suicide can be at all romantic) method would be to weigh down my pockets with stones and walk into the sea à la Virginia Woolf—but my death has no need for literary statements.

None of these methods is right for me. I know what I'll choose. I will slice my wrists. I read that you don't cut the inside surface, but the upper edge, where you feel a pulse. A sharp blade—my husband uses straight razor blades when he wallpapers—will evoke little pain. Then you just rest and let the life flow out, like menses, just another part of the eternal cycle. Such a relief, such peace. That's all I want—peace.

I couldn't do this at home. I wouldn't want my family to find me. I'll drive to my favorite spot, the beach—the sacred portal to the universe. No one would be there this time of year. At dawn, with the huge orange sun hinting at its plans, I'll brave the cold water barefoot and memorize the squish of sand like powder between my toes. I'll collect shells—clams, mussels, oysters, snails, scallops—and search the surf for a sand shark, remembering how Collin used to catch them barehanded, play with them in a pail, then throw them back. Finally, I'll sit on the cool sand just above the water's edge, let the salt tighten my face, and breathe in the briny bouquet. A Greek chorus of professional mourners will gather at a respectful distance, their squawks and caws a psychic wall around me. As the tide begins to encroach, I'll drink in one last image of the world and its sense and nonsense. It is time.

I tremble as the blade parts skin, flesh, vessel—a sensual, almost orgasmic release. A chill washes over me as life draws the last energy from its host. Will I see the white light or simply fall unconscious? My mind's eye takes in the tide already stretching toward me, lusting after the élan vital that flows black in the half-light, carrying it back to the earth. The pain is gone—

No . . . no! The beach would be forever tainted. My family could never again enjoy riding boogie boards over the waves or smooshing their toes through the burning sand to the cool underneath or being lulled to sleep by the narcotic sun and rhythmic lap-lap-lapping. It can't be the beach. Besides, it's too public. Someone would surely rescue me.

I sigh. My dog Maggie climbs up on the bed. She licks the salt from my face and curls into a ball, nestled against me. Does she know what I'm planning? She reads my body language all the time, knowing whether I'm going out or whether I might be receptive to her "please" face and give her a treat. She can always tell when I'm sick. It's been tough on her these past few weeks, with me Jekyll-and-Hyde-ing between zombie and banshee. I scooch down and bury my face in her soft fur, and the tears return.

I want to die. I really, really do. I'm not afraid of death—its threat pales beside the desperation of this mother's grief. Oh, death has power. And it's sly—the pain it inflicts on the living muddles the mind until it seems no longer a choice but a must. If suicide were easier, didn't require so much forethought and technical planning, I might already be gone.

Death already showed its best cards. There's nothing worse it can do to me.

My vulnerable moment has passed and reason has reclaimed the remote. I feel ashamed of my cowardly longing. This death-wish must ever remain a fantasy I indulge for the vicarious, momentary liberation it provides. Wasn't it Nietszche who said the thought of suicide could get you through a dark night?[27] How hurt would my loved ones be, assuming that loving them wasn't enough for me—that they weren't enough? I can't ease my heart without tearing out theirs. Death would transfer my pain to those I love—and I love them too much to inflict this agony. They are everything. I've always known I would do anything for my children. Now I know what anything is.

---

[27] "The thought of suicide is a strong consolation: by means of it one gets through many a dark night." –Friedrich Nietzsche

Soft laughter and the gentle clang of pots and pans waft from below. I scratch Maggie's belly and wipe my eyes. She jumps up, wags her butt, and herds me downstairs.

IX
Back to the Future

I smiled today
—and whined and frowned and railed and
cried,
but those are old frenemies.
A smile is a new beau.

Resignation

*A*cceptance: the final stage of grief (if you believe it has stages). The final exam before summer vacation. The last dragon to slay before happily ever after. One should approach eagerly, ready to shuck the oppressive cloak that has muffled life's expression for so long. So why must I be dragged to acceptance kicking and cursing?

The word *acceptance* itself presents a formidable hurdle. It is not the correct word to define this reality. The *American Heritage Dictionary* defines acceptance as:

1) The act or process of accepting.
2) The state of being accepted or acceptable.
3) Favorable reception; approval.
4) Belief in something; agreement.

Acceptance implies going along willingly, tacit agreement that this is how things should be. I will never *accept* my son's death. I may, however, reach a point at which I resign myself that he has died.

Perhaps you're rolling your eyes and saying this is semantics—needless haggling over minute differences in meaning. Or you may interpret acceptance the same way I do yet not understand the differences between the words. But to me, words possess sacred and magical power—they constitute a force akin to gravity or electromagnetism.

The infinite subtle distinctions among English synonyms are delightful. Everyone "knows" Eskimos have dozens of words for snow, but few realize the *Oxford English Dictionary* has 125 snow-related words. There is a reason dictionaries contain *blithe, exultant, delighted,* and *contented* as well as *happy.* Who would characterize Santa as *rapturous* or Saint Francis's prayer as *jolly?* Finding a word with the right rhythm, inflection, and nuance is an emotional thrill. So when words are used inappropriately to describe something as personal as grief, and I'm expected to endorse the concept, I resist both on principle and as a matter of practicality.

Grief books embrace the term *acceptance* because of the word's positive connotations. Rather than an accidental choice, embracing *acceptance* is a purposeful, subtle psychological strategy of giving the bereaved a positive goal. Elisabeth Kübler-Ross, arguably the first to suggest stages of grief in her book, *On Death and Dying,* coined the terms as stages of dying. She eventually published *On Grief and Grieving,* acknowledging that dying is akin to grieving in advance. Kübler-Ross's experience suggested that a terminal patient who accepts death as an upcoming adventure may make an easier transition than one who resigns himself or herself to an inability to halt the process.

Similarly, a bereaved person who looks ahead to acceptance subconsciously processes all of the word's implied meanings, while one who looks forward to resignation after the knock-down-drag-out quadruple-punch of shock, anger, bargaining, and depression sees a less rosy future. Pollyannaish self-delusion of acceptance may help some grievers. If the goal is not desirable, why work to get there?

The problem with such misrepresentation is that *acceptance* gives people the wrong idea about loss. Those who have never suffered intense grief get the message that the suffering soon ends and everything is fine and dandy again. When they later experience loss, they don't understand why they don't feel all better and wonder if they are abnormal. Friends become impatient with their inability to return to "normal."

Even professional therapists sometimes bulldoze grievers into moving on. Psychiatrists made me feel worse, not better. Just six weeks after Collin's death, a therapist told me to get over it—do some volunteer work.

Thus the bereaved must fight extra battles when they are least equipped to do so. Society loses, too, in trying to enforce unnatural expectations. Although most psychologists agree acute grief lasts three to five years, the average length of funeral leave, according to the U.S. Bureau of Labor Statistics, is 3.7 days.

Unexpressed or unremarked grief may emerge as somatic or mental illness, causing lost work productivity and cultural participation as well as individual and family problems. Rituals that acknowledge death and mourning are part of the fabric that holds a group together. A community that treats death as irrelevant soon fails to value life.

It wasn't always this way. When families were larger and antibiotics still a dream, death was part of American life. Everyone had lost someone—a child, a sibling, a parent, a friend—and they rallied to help one another process the complex emotions of grief. People died at home, rather than in hospitals, and loved ones cared for them and prepared their bodies for burial.

Now, we wash our hands instead of our loved ones, leaving preparations to funeral directors, and sometimes forego viewings or even funerals. No longer community experiences, death and grief have become private affairs.

Other cultures—ironically, ones we smugly consider less advanced—retain community traditions and rituals that comfort the bereaved. On the Day of the Dead, Mexicans remember and pray for friends and family members who have died. Survivors dance and sing, celebrate the lives of their loved ones, tell stories about them, prepare their favorite foods, and decorate altars in their honor.

In Vietnam, close friends and relatives bring flowers and incense to the cemetery three days after a funeral. Every seventh day for the next forty-nine days, they hold a memorial, at which they pray, share a meal, and reminisce. Successive memorials are held on the hundredth day after death, on the one-year anniversary, and a year after that.

Whether or not the support of community rituals is available, each bereaved person must meet the final stage of grief on his or her own terms. Some may find they *do* accept—for them, the word is accurate. For the remainder, however, a more appropriate and realistic designation would be *resignation*. Other apt terms include *surrender, acquiescence, capitulation, concession,* and *submission,* which imply resistance to acceptance. Such terms conjure images of military surrenders: Robert E. Lee did not accept the North's moral superiority, but grudgingly conceded that the South could not prevail. I do not agree Collin should have died, but I acknowledge that I cannot bring him back.

Acceptance also implies putting the bad behind you, which presupposes severing the bond with the deceased. This alienation is still a problem if it is called *resignation*. Those who face loss must rant and rail and rend their clothes and exhort their beloveds to, as poet Dylan Thomas urged, "not go gentle into that good night." Even a foe recognized as unbeatable must be challenged. Acknowledgment of grief reaffirms the deceased's importance to the bereaved and the community, asserting that his or her life had meaning. I betray my son if I give up too soon.

Resignation must evolve slowly, naturally—an existence one realizes only later to have achieved. Thus the last stage of grief is not something to look forward to, but to be tardily grateful for, as one who is devastated at getting fired but later lands the job of his or her dreams.

I am not sure whether I have reached resignation. I acknowledge academically that no miracle will bring Collin back to life; my anguish has abated. But I still hope a stone will lodge in the cogs of the universe, opening a door through which Collin will cross back home, and I hold grief and its accomplice, depression, at bay only with the big stick of medication.

Perhaps this is as good as it gets. Perhaps to expect more would require acceptance.

Do It

*A*uthor Hope Edelman wrote after her mother's death, "Loss is our legacy. Insight is our gift. Memory is our guide." More a Marine drill instructor—or sometimes a Nazi commandant—than a guide, grief orders us to *do* something. Author Anne Rice immortalized her daughter Michele as the beautiful vampire child Claudia in *Interview with the Vampire*. After the abduction and death of his son, John Walsh began a crusade for justice as host of TV's *America's Most Wanted*. Our friends Don and Jeanne founded atTAcK Addiction, an advocacy and support group, to honor their son Tyler and prevent other parents from experiencing the pain of losing a child to opioid addiction. I've written this account of my son's death and my grief.

The doing need not be so conspicuous, however. It may be as simple as telling a child her grandmother's stories, or funding a scholarship in a friend's name, or sharing our insights so others don't mourn alone. But we must each do the action that only we can, rubbing out grief's fingerprints with our own.

Tupperware

One April afternoon, I stood at the sink and rinsed the big blue Tupperware popcorn bowl, a remnant of the previous night's butter fix. Better than Prozac, butter, if a bit short-lived. Ironically, the bowl's cheery plastic seemed to ground me—Gaia's armor against the mystical conundrums that rained like missiles. I closed my eyes as they surged again—death-questions; soul-questions; God-questions. The sponge read the bumps in the bowl, pits burned by betrayed kernels, as if feeling for the answers in Braille. Rain pattered on the roof and my eyes traced tears that crawled down the porch screen. The corners of my mouth turned up. The gloom suited me.

I had slept 'til noon, no telemarketers plucking me from the morning dream-chase that ended a wide-eyed night of infomercials, the *Crocodile Hunter*, and a B—no, C—movie on SciFi. Drowsing another hour, I held off the day's demands—bills to pay and Hamburger Helper to cook. Next I showered, standing mesmerized under the water until my trust ran out, and then washed, brushed my teeth, and let the water beat on my back until it turned on me.

Wrapped in my terrycloth robe, I poured iced tea and toasted English muffins—extra butter in the nooks and crannies—and kept tabs on the rain out of the corner of my eye as I read the paper. Unable to move to the next activity, I read it all, even the parts I usually skipped—the weather and the local calendar and the sports section.

A stack of bills peeked out from under the *News Journal*. Metaphysical clouds in my head repulsed the numbers' rational, linear coldness. I tidied the pile, wiped fingerprints off the fridge, swept up the doggie tumbleweeds, and made a new pitcher of iced tea. Finally I shoved the bills into the kitchen drawer and did the dishes.

As I gave the popcorn bowl a final rinse, something occurred to me: I did my best housecleaning when avoiding other, more odious, tasks. Another idea insinuated itself into my soul. An answer. It didn't so much grow as become, and I didn't so much think of it as become surrounded by it. The sensation was a soft discernment; a gentle awareness; a gift.

The realization floated diaphanous, gossamer, but I didn't need arguments or proofs or confirmation. I just knew it was so—Collin was safe.

That single nugget of intuition turned a tumbler in the lock of grief's prison. I felt a perceptible lightening—long-captive breath released; jaws unlocked; cataracts thinned. The moment would have been dramatic had the rain stopped, but it hadn't. It suited me. It pleased me, too, that the knowledge had come, not on a sun-slathered beach, or at work, or in a church, but in my heart's kitchen.

Several months passed before I received the next number in the combination. As before, this new realization caressed me hello, but didn't fall from heaven. I had worked for understanding, invited enlightenment, and built upon the initial insight by investing my whole being into reading books and thinking and talking with friends and debating in my journal. I trust that perseverance and grace will uncover more even as I suspect a lengthy incarceration.

In *Mysticism: The Nature and Development of Spiritual Consciousness*, Evelyn Underhill likened mystics to solitary crusaders: "He goes because he must, as Galahad went towards the Grail: knowing that for those who can live it, this alone is life." So with mourners: I grieve because I must. Understanding is my grail. And for now at least, this crusade is my life.

Epilogue

A soft vroom signals the truck's approach. The mailbox door snaps open and closed, and the engine accelerates to the next house. Sighing, I consider whether to drag my cement boots the thirty-nine steps (oh, yes, I've counted them) to the box, trudge the thirty-nine steps back (Is there something Freudian in the allusion to Hitchcock's man on the run?), then tear open the envelopes and become buried in an avalanche of bills, notices, and junk. Today it feels like too much work and too much negative emotion to endure.

I didn't get the mail yesterday either. Ed might grab it today when he comes home from work—or maybe tomorrow. Sometimes the box doesn't get emptied until it is stuffed full. Then the correspondence piles up on the counter until I'm mentally ready to deal with it. Long ago, Ed took over paying the bills.

Multiple responsibilities enervate me. A Type A striver in my previous life, I juggled a dozen tasks at once and thrived on the adventure, embracing Helen Keller's idea that "Life is either a daring adventure, or nothing." I was always in the thick of things. If there was a discussion, I was in it. If there was an organization, I was president. In school, I was in band, chorus, tennis, student council, honor society, to name just a few.

As a teacher, I led workshops, took my students to competitions, and organized school events. My principal called me one of her "crazies," her movers and shakers. When the district superintendent came to a faculty meeting, I chose the seat next to him. One of the teachers said, "We all knew you'd sit there." My dad had been a superintendent, so I held no awe for authority figures—the old "he puts on his pants one leg at a time." But my colleagues saw me as fearless.

I maintained the same level of engagement with my family. I initiated a "special day" for each of the kids, giving each my undivided attention without the other kids along. Matt and I went to Gettysburg, Collin and I to the Maryland Science Center, and Katie and I to the Smithsonian. And I was spontaneous. When fifth-grade Katie was assigned a report on Vermont, we dropped everything and drove there from Delaware for the weekend.

After burying Collin, I buried myself. Now, instead of jumping into the action, I watch from the sidelines, keeping my distance, keeping my own counsel, keeping others at arms' length. I've stuffed myself into one of those novelty Sumo wrestler inflatables, and I bounce off things, but nothing can touch me. Besides, nothing seems important enough for me to offer my two cents. I have nothing to say. I can go days without needing to talk to anyone. Ed is a talker, so it drives him crazy.

Then there's the energy issue. It's just too exhausting to get involved. It takes a supreme act of will to haul myself out of bed each morning. I wake up bone-weary and heave a big Eeyore[28] sigh. I consider starting the day, then roll up in the covers, wrap my arms around myself, and float back into my dreams. Heavy blankets provide comforting weight, an inverse "Princess and the Pea" scenario. Usually it's a screaming bladder that finally ejects me from my cocoon. Sometimes I get up and pee and then dive back under the covers.

Once I get going I manage, but everything is an effort. More sighs while I shower and do my morning ablutions in slow motion. I fritter a lot of time reading the news and deleting spam emails. Having even a few items on my unwritten to-do list paralyzes me or I perseverate, clicking on page after Google page or editing a single sentence to death. Being involved brings responsibilities and choices and demands I can't fulfill. It disappoints others and embarrasses me. I know my limits. I didn't used to have any.

Losing this part of myself has been painful. No one was more shocked than I when this control freak lost all control. I was proud to call myself a problem solver, steely in a crisis and clearheaded in

---

[28] The depressed donkey character from *Winnie-the-Pooh*.

identifying what needed to be done. Before Collin died, if asked how I would deal with my child's death, I'd have said I'd grieve deeply, then find new meaning and move on with life. I could never have fathomed losing two decades to Grief. But I didn't know Grief very well then.

We have a party to attend tonight, so I'm already psyching myself up to vomit smiles and small talk. Social situations require me to crawl from my cocoon and pretend everything is okay. It's exhausting. Happy used to be so easy. A fellow teacher once told me she pulled up next to my car at a red light and envied the way my kids and I laughed and sang. At least tonight's party is a family get-together. Being around my aunts and cousins usually gives me a lift.

Collin died twenty-two years ago. He would be thirty-nine now, but in my mind he is frozen at just shy of seventeen. It is difficult to envision what his life might have become. Surely someone with the personal motto "Never Give Up" would have achieved his dream of announcing for ESPN. I hope he would have married and had children. Mostly I envision him as happy.

I embarked on this book eighteen years ago. It has taken me that long to gain some perspective and to discern which of my musings would appeal to readers. And it just takes a long time when you are depressed and must flee the grief tornadoes that touch down when revisiting painful events. Some entries were written long ago, while others are more recent additions. Thus, you follow my grief's evolution. A long, tedious process, it has yet been the seminal creative accomplishment of my life.

Although writing this book has helped me, it hasn't vanquished my grief. I still actively mourn my son. Deep grief—some psychologists call it complicated grief—does not simply disappear. The Mayo Clinic describes complicated grief as "feelings of loss [that] are debilitating and don't improve even after time passes." It may affect more than twenty percent of bereaved parents, especially mothers.[29] But dealing with it is a challenge because no one agrees on what "normal" grief is, or that normal even exists. Everyone grieves differently.

---

[29] Andrea Volpe, "The People Who Can't Stop Grieving," *Independent* (Nov. 15, 2016), Retrieved September 22 from https://www.independent.co.uk/life-style/health-and-families/people-who-can-t-stop-grieving-science-mourning-psychologists-a7416116.html.

Complicated grief is usually treated with cognitive behavioral therapy (CBT), which I have done for many years. A new technique, complicated grief therapy (CGT), combines CBT and exposure therapy. In ever-increasing doses, patients confront the stories and situations that inform their grief. I'm not sure how this works, as I confront my grief every day.

Some therapists want complicated grief added to the Diagnostic and Statistical Manual (DSM), the bible of mental disorders, because without a listing, insurance companies will not reimburse treatment. Many do what my doctors did—call it depression, which is listed. But as someone who continues to experience both, I can state categorically—they are not the same. I would love to cure my depression, and it would be great to have more energy and to better handle difficult situations. But my raw grief feels like a natural response to loss. Grief is intertwined with love—a sort of Grief Stockholm Syndrome. I am bereft because I loved—still love—so deeply. Should we want to take that away?

I despise the old adage "time heals." I'm positive it was coined by people who never experienced loss and wanted their bereaved loved ones to get back to "normal." Rose Kennedy, who bore the deaths of four of her nine children, as well as several grandchildren and great-grandchildren, remarked: "It has been said that time heals all wounds. I don't agree. The wounds remain. Time—the mind, protecting its sanity—covers them with some scar tissue and the pain lessens, but it is never gone." My grief-wound will never heal because my love for Collin will never end. Time may alleviate my suffering even as it holds hostage both my son and the woman I used to be. I have wrestled my pain into a sort of submission that lets me cope in the world, and I save my tears for the shower and my pillow and smile on cue.

But I am still broken. Just because I am used to grief doesn't mean it has stopped hurting. I never returned to teaching young children, as I no longer have the emotional strength or stamina to fulfill their needs and can only manage a few hours of focused work a day. Weaseling onto the easier path, I pursued a master's degree and then taught university-level creative writing and composition. The part-time position allowed me to indulge my love of teaching without feeling overwhelmed, as twice a week I taught two classes and then went home.

It's not that I feel sad all the time. I've reached a stalemate with grief, but depression still has the upper hand. Today my biggest challenge is generating and maintaining energy. Antidepressants and transcranial magnetic stimulation (TMS) shield me from despair but don't keep me on an even keel, so I use food to help regulate my mood. Predictably, my weight has crept ever higher. Exercise is said to relieve depression, so sometimes I hit tennis balls against a wall, but when turning over in bed takes an act of will, walking is such an effort it makes me feel worse. Because no medicinal magic has regenerated my former energy and motivation, I never know what I'll be able to cope with on any given day.

Making decisions can be hard—even things as innocuous as what to cook for dinner or which craft to do with the kids can leave me paralyzed. Phone calls are especially stressful—sometimes it takes me ages to make an appointment or call a friend. Recently, my doctor and I played telephone tag. It's been a month and I still haven't called him back. I'd like to check in with friends but can't make myself pick up the phone. I recently learned that there's a name for feeling overwhelmed by choices and changes—decision fatigue. It's a real thing.

Grief gets in the way of things that should be fun. I used to schedule social events with friends every weekend, but now we only see our family. Sometimes Ed and I enjoy an impromptu night out, but planning is difficult because I never know whether I'll be up to making the effort. And when I do put myself into such situations, I need time to decompress afterward, alone with no responsibilities. So mostly we just stay home. Although I used to hate the wasteland that is regular TV—thousands of channels and nothing worth watching—now Ed sits in the recliner and I recline on the couch, and we lose ourselves in one of a half-dozen series we've recorded.

As I write this, we are in the throes of the COVID-19 quarantine. I have to admit that not being allowed to go anywhere has been a relief rather than a burden. But the longer we isolate ourselves, the more I slip back into that safe, comfortable place inside my head, disappearing into solitary pursuits like reading, writing, crosswords, crafts, Facebook, and late-night episodes of *House Hunters*. Ed bought me noise-canceling headphones so I could listen to music or the TV at night without disturbing his sleep. He didn't realize they would offer another way for me to erase the world.

I wasn't blessed with my dad's and Ed's ability to talk to anyone, anywhere, but before Collin died I felt confident and was good at chatting and schmoozing with my colleagues, my students' parents and my clients. But grief stunted my people skills. A decade ago, I attended a number of networking events to try to kick off my editing business. I hated making small talk, hated feeling like everyone could see what a hot mess I was. I walked with my head down, hoping no one would notice me. Then afterward, I was upset no one had talked to me. A year ago, I did better, visiting libraries, classrooms, bookstores, and festivals to promote my children's book, *When Poke Woke*. Now I feel like I've regressed.

Sorry to be such a downer. I've tried all sorts of strategies to kick the monster, including exercise, meditation, positive affirmations, and gratitude, and although they help for a moment, I can't sustain the feelings. I even attended a jumpstart-your-life weekend workshop. The life coach was positive he could cure my grief. He had me stand in front of the group while he lectured me and asked me questions. I should have refused to participate, but too beaten down to resist, I endured it, tears streaming down my face. "Would your son want you to live life like this?" he asked, the single most inane question you can ask a bereaved parent. Of course Collin wouldn't want this for me. *I* don't want this for me. I'm ready to enjoy life again—I've been ready for years. Academically, I can envision a different life. I just can't figure out how to make it happen.

Please know that all this soul-baring is not a plea for sympathy. My hope is that instead, I've evoked your *empathy* for everyone shattered by devastating loss. Until I experienced it, I thought grief was just sadness. I had no idea how debilitating it could be, how long it could last, or that it could change my entire personality. Even if you've experienced grief, know that it is an emotional continuum. Each of us experiences loss individually, and every death affects us differently. It's not a competition—no "my grief is worse than yours." But some losses damage us more deeply than others. The deaths of my favorite uncle, beloved grandmother, and dear parents hit hard, but they did not change my life. The death of my son, however, triggered a never-ending avalanche.

I want others who experience this to know they are not weird or crazy or selfish. They do not need to be fixed, only to be loved and supported. I want those who care about them to be compassionate.

When your sister can't bear the thought of enduring your bachelorette weekend, or your best friend bails at the last minute even though the concert tickets cost $300, realize that it isn't about you. They are doing what they must to survive. And remember to talk about the person who died—say his or her name.

Although deep grief casts a huge shadow over everything, it's not all doom and gloom—light pierces the darkness periodically. Every once in a while, a day will greet me with balloons, the lead blanket will lift, and my old spirit will waltz back into my flesh, the way the ghosts in *Beetlejuice* slammed into and took over characters' bodies. Sometimes antidepressants give me a few weeks or months of relief. When that happens, I become a whirlwind—catching up on errands and cleaning, writing, and beginning new creative projects without a moment's thought—until the meds stop working and the walls close back in.

Progress has been a jagged path that trends uphill. I'm stronger than I was five years ago; more engaged with others than I was ten years ago; and functional today, whereas twenty years ago, I spent days swaddled in my bed. When grief was new, I couldn't focus to read or write. Though I stared at the TV, I couldn't have told you whether I was watching *The Simpsons* or *The X-Files*. Seeing Kraft mac and cheese in the Acme would trigger a breakdown in aisle five.

Now books are my favorite escape, and I have time to read things that interest and inspire me. Playing guitar and flute, painting and doing crafts, walking and hitting tennis balls nurtures my soul. I'm able to write at least a few hours a week. My editing work helps others become their own best selves, and I hope my books will do the same. I've even made a few new friends. I feed my passion to teach by conducting writing workshops and by sharing *When Poke Woke* with children. Still a night owl, I sleep late when I can, diminishing the amount of day I must plod through, but I rarely lie down during daytime hours. And Kraft mac and cheese evokes memories of Collin that wrap themselves around me like a dog's ThunderShirt.

My friend Michelle asked about my vision for my "best life," and I responded that I am living it. I'm pretty sure I shocked her since she had just supported me through a difficult March. It stunned me too, as the feeling had swirled in my consciousness for some time, but I hadn't acknowledged it. The black hole of Collin's absence looms over my world, and I teeter on the event horizon,[30] alternately struggling to avoid slipping over the edge and leaning back to freefall into the void. But I am resigned to this backdrop and no longer beat myself up if I feel like a dishrag for several days in a row. Except for the ever-present depression and lack of energy, my life is good, and I am . . . happy.

I can't quite believe I just wrote that. It's the first time I've even thought it since Collin died. I've always looked at grief as a zero-sum game—either I can grieve or I can be happy. But it seems I can do both simultaneously. Beneath my ever-present Mary Poopins grief umbrella, I am happy to read, write, teach, and be creative; help make other people's lives better; and love and be loved. Maybe it's not a happy you would be satisfied with, but it's the closest I've come.

An amazing support system helped bring me to this place. Ed's and my parents were constant presences, quietly cheering in the background and keeping the family running. They helped with household chores and family obligations and buoyed us emotionally.

My parents were well-acquainted with grief. Mom lost her beloved father while she was in college, and she and my dad buried a stillborn son. Dad shepherded three of his sisters through the deaths of their young husbands. Collin's death devastated my parents. Except when his mother died, it was the only time I'd ever seen my dad cry. My mom told me that even worse than her own grief was seeing me so shattered. She couldn't finish an early draft of this manuscript. Having grown up during the Depression and come of age during World War II, my parents were from the school of pick yourself up, dust yourself off, then get on with life. Still, neither tried to tell me how to grieve or to get on with things. They just provided absolute love.

All our parents have gone to be with Collin, but cherished friends, along with my sister, brother, cousins, and aunts, continue to wrap me in their selfless love. Matt stops by just to chat, and it feels like the happy old days. Katie is my best friend. The children's antics and repartee keep us all laughing through Sunday dinners. I get to hug my darlings and read, write, and play with them—reveling in their

---

[30] The edge of a black hole.

unabashed delight as they discover that robin eggs are the most glorious shade of blue, ice cream cones are geometric shapes, and becoming a teenager opens the door to a whole new world.

Ed and I have reached that comfortable, contented stage in our marriage that we call "beyond love." We draw comfort and strength from each other. He makes me feel safe when Grief tightens the noose. If I could lose a hundred pounds, gain some energy, and get Collin back, life would be perfect.

The biggest turning point in my grief journey came unanticipated and had nothing to do with mourning. After a decade wondering whether I would ever truly smile again, the births of my niece and grandchildren rekindled my joy. There is no more comforting, all-is-right-with-the-world feeling than holding a sleeping baby. Author Anne Lamott writes that "a baby feels and smells like God." If that's the closest I get to God, I'll be satisfied. Seeing the kids' faces light up as they ride a merry-go-round (or soar over fences on a real horse), hearing their delighted squeals as they jump the waves, and snuggling together to share our beloved books transport me to a world beyond sadness and pain. Plus, being there for them completely is kind of a do-over for me, atonement for being AWOL when Katie and Matt needed me.

Once I tame Lethargy, the giant wolf-dog with its paws on my chest, maybe I will be able to report that I have turned the final corner and am doing well. Then I will be able to do more than exist. For everyone dies, but not everyone lives. Collin lived.

Until we meet again, Collin—your tomorrow. You are worth every tear.

Cherry Blossoms

The hospital floats in the gray,
empty-armed comfort cold
as the tile. Snow gathers
on the sill, and wool and fleece hide
my shivering.

A wary chrysalid, I emerge
among cherry blossoms that have appeared—abracadabra!
—like a magician's fluffy creatures parading
their new spring line with the cotton-candy smiles
of those who know they are beautiful;
each passing my secret to the next, snickering
at my bare-faced pain.
Crows queue in the furrows of my face as I squint,
SPF-less, against color's stealth assault; pulse after pulse burning,
a laser peel tattooing
me with pigment only hollowed eyes can feel.

Hungry to celebrate, perhaps the deb-blossoms suck
the life pulsing from me, glorying
in their moment, as did I. Amid arms
reaching, fingers beckoning me to the dance,
I recoil from the flames
licking my soul, their crackling percussion a solo
riff mute against the dirge—you marching,
not to your own drummer, but in your own band;
Closing the show opening
night.

Another spring, another strike; life's gloat
a minefield blossoming
before me. Bunting cradled
in old crone arms—the old welcoming
the new—is out of place here,
color blanched, beauty diminished
by what has gone.
For beauty is nothing
without love—Rapunzel locked

in a tower, a prince trapped
within a beast, a supermodel washing her hair
on Saturday night.
Each bud kisses the breeze openmouthed
in a promise of forever, then flies,
enjoying the tease; perhaps
this world is not as promised—
or a better gig awaits. Their thorns pierce
the silken breastplate of my heart in uncountable tiny pricks.

A nickel of years now,
and the flowers return
for their yearly performance. My armor is thicker; empty
channels bracketed by heavy-wale corduroy bend and crush, but hold;
only fragrance squeezes through, prodding primal
instinct, superseding rational thought.
Color returns as if we have landed
in Oz.
A new landscape of cherry trees lines the brick road, their pink cloud
batting
the boundary between here and after, re-embracing
without apology their fifteen minutes of fame;
And I am struck
that they live a lifetime
in a day and are grateful
for the dream booking. Perhaps loveliness is perversely
proportional to fragility—the more intense
for its concentrated burst.
Like you.

I never noticed before—
each bloom wears the velvety memory
of your skin, and your name skips
on each fluttering whisper;
you did not flout the season
of rebirth, but were delivered to the universe
by celestial midwives; your supernova after-image a billboard
promise of a return
engagement.

So lovely, the cherry blossoms . . .

Acknowledgments

Loving thanks to all who helped, supported, encouraged, and tolerated me as I prepared this manuscript.

Diane Penrod, my graduate program advisor, helped me shape and focus disparate ideas into a single work and provided the objective judgment that ensured individual pieces were appropriate and meaningful.

Julia Chang, my academic thesis advisor, taught me to use figurative language and to let action and sensory input, rather than thought and abstraction, dominate my work. She helped me trust my writing and respect readers enough to excise second and third explanations that the teacher in me kept sneaking into the narrative.

Sanford Tweedie introduced me to multi-genre writing and facilitated a class environment that invited and rewarded originality and risk. Along with Julia, Sandy held my hand as I took my first baby steps across the lawn of metaphor.

Editor Patti Cleary helped me reframe the chapters and pointed out what was missing in this manuscript, what needed to be cut, and where I needed to go into more detail. She provided invaluable advice about what publishers are looking for. Her generous compliments of my metaphors and stories were delightful pep talks that kept me moving forward.

My lifelong friend Gail Chupein and cousin Kim Stitik enthusiastically volunteered to read my manuscript, as did Kelly Kotte Pharis, Penny Rogers, Munchie Morgan Clement, and Thomasine Smith Bianchi, members of my local Facebook support group, Hockessin Understands Grief (HUG). Each beta reader offered unique feedback, caught errors, and reassured me that my story wasn't just one big whine-fest. Their input was invaluable.

Artist extraordinaire Ezequiel Decarli graciously interrupted his work on *Poke's Toque* to design this book's cover. The illustration perfectly captures the mood of the story and the idea of Collin soaring among the stars.

My parents, Nancy and George Glynn, are gone now, but they would likely be more proud of this book than I. They instilled in me a love of learning and helped me develop the skills I needed to persevere and succeed. By example, they showed me how to set the bar high and know that I could do anything I wanted. Their unwavering pride in me continues to be my "eagle's wings."

My children, Matthew, Collin, and Katie, and my grandchildren and niece have evoked in me a love and joy I never imagined was possible, which sustains me through the despair and desiccation of grief. Also to my delight, Katie, whom I taught to write, now points out my mixed metaphors and poor transitions. She, along with my sister, Kelly Glynn, and lifelong family friend Judy Austin, provided invaluable early editorial comment and copyediting. Thanks also to Matt, Katie, and my husband, Ed, for allowing their grief experiences to be a part of this work.

Ed never gave up on me when I checked out from life. He encouraged me to enroll in the Master of Writing program that ignited this book, even though it strained our finances and made him Atlas, bearing the burden of our family's support on his shoulders. He never complained as two years stretched to three or when writing sessions left him to fix dinner or sleep alone. My forever love, Ed encourages me when I doubt and is my staunch and vocal champion.

Finally, a mountain of thanks to everyone who reached out to or supported my family and me in the dark days after Collin's death, as well as those who continue to shower us with affection and blessings and say Collin's name.

To all of you, my sincerest thanks, gratitude, and love.

Susan

Resources

Beyond Death

Altea, Rosemary. *The Eagle and the Rose*. New York: Warner, 1995.

Anderson, George, and Andrew Barone. *George Anderson's Lessons from the Light: Extraordinary Messages of Comfort and Hope from the Other Side*. New York: Berkeley, 1999.

Browne, Sylvia. *The Other Side and Back: A Psychic's Guide to Our World and Beyond*. New York: Dutton, 1999.

Eadie, Betty J. *Embraced by the Light*. Placerville, CA: Gold Leaf Press, 1992.

Edward, John. *One Last Time: A Psychic Medium Speaks to Those We Have Loved and Lost*. New York: Berkeley, 1998.

Moody, Raymond. *Life After life: The Investigation of a Phenomenon — Survival of Bodily Death*. Mechanicsburg, PA: Stackpole, 1976.

Van Praagh, James. *Talking to Heaven: A Medium's Message of Life After Death*. New York: Dutton, 1997.

Weiss, Brian L. *Many Lives, Many Masters*. New York: Fireside, 1988.

Grief

Edelman, Hope. *Motherless Daughters: The Legacy of Loss*. Addlestone, Surrey, England: Delta, 1995.

Finkbeiner, Anne K. *After the Death of a Child: Living with Loss Through the Years*. Baltimore, MD: Johns Hopkins Press, 1994.

Gorer, Geoffrey. *Death, Grief and Mourning*. New York: Arno, 1977.

Kübler-Ross, Elisabeth. *On Death and Dying.* New York: Touchstone, 1969.

———. *On Grief and Grieving.* New York: Scribner, 2005.

Lewis, C. S. *A Grief Observed.* New York: HarperOne, 2009.

Manning, Doug. *Don't Take My Grief Away.* San Francisco: HarperCollins, 1979.

McCracken, Amy, and Mary Semel (Eds.). *A Broken Heart Still Beats After Your Child Dies.* Center City, MN: Hazelden, 1998.

Religion

Bahm, Archie. J. *The World's Living Religions.* Berkeley, CA: Asian Humanities Press, 1992.

Browne, Sylvia. "About Novus," 2002. Retrieved March 21, 2003, from http://www.sylvia.org/home/aboutnovus/cfm.

Cooper, David A. *God is a Verb: Kabbalah and the Practice of Mystical Judaism.* New York: Riverhead, 1997.

Holmes, Ernest. *Science of Mind: A Philosophy, a Faith, a Way of Life.* New York: Putnam, 1938.

Kiefert, William C. *Why Are Gnostic Teachings Missing?* 2001. Retrieved March 21, 2003, from http://www.gnosticchristianity.com/frameset_CH8.htm.

The Nexus of Science and Spirituality

Borysenko, Joan. *A Woman's Book of Life: The Biology, Psychology, and the Spirituality of the Feminine Life Cycle.* New York: Riverhead, 1998.

Glynn, Patrick. *God: The Evidence—The Reconciliation of Faith and Reason in a Postsecular World.* Rocklin, CA: Forum, 1997.

Hunt, Valerie V. *Infinite Mind: Science of the Human Vibrations of Consciousness*. Malibu, CA: Malibu Publishing, 1996.

Katra, Jane, and Russell Targ. *The Heart of the Mind: How to Experience God Without Belief*. Novato, Cal.: New World Library, 2000.

Newberg, Andrew, Eugene D'Aquili, and Vince Rause. *Why God Won't Go Away: Brain Science and the Biology of Belief*. New York: Ballantine, 2001.

Sheldrake, Rupert. *Dogs that Know When Their Owners Are Coming Home: And Other Unexplained Powers of Animals*. New York: Crown, 1999.

The Dalai Lama. *The Universe in a Single Atom: The Convergence of Science and Spirituality*. New York: Harmony, 2006.

Wilber, Ken. *The Marriage of Sense and Soul: Integrating Science and Religion*. New York: Random House, 1998.

Spiritual Healing

Brennan, Barbara A. *Hands of Light: A Guide to Healing Through the Human Energy Field*. New York: Bantam, 1987.

Bruyere, Rosalyn L. *Wheels of Light: Chakras, Auras, and Healing Energy of the Body*. New York: Fireside, 1994.

Dossey, Larry. *Prayer is Good Medicine: How to Reap the Healing Benefits of Prayer*. San Francisco: HarperSanFrancisco, 1996.

Matthews, Dale A. *The Faith Factor: Proof of the Healing Power of Prayer*. New York: Viking, 1998.

Myss, Caroline. *Anatomy of the Spirit: The Seven Stages of Power and Healing*. New York: Three Rivers Press, 1996.

Schulz, Mona Lisa. *Awakening Intuition: Using Your Mind-body Network for Insight and Healing*. New York: Harmony, 1998.

Siegel, Bernie S. *Love, Medicine and Miracles: Lessons Learned About Self-healing from a Surgeon's Experience with Exceptional Patients*. New York: HarperPerennial, 1986.

Spirituality

Borysenko, Joan. *A Woman's Journey to God: Finding the Feminine Path.* New York: Riverhead, 1999.

———. *The Ways of the Mystic: Seven Paths to God*. Carlsbad, CA: Hay House, 1997.

Harris, Sam. *Waking Up: A Guide to Spirituality Without Religion.* New York: Simon and Schuster, 2015.

Walsch, Neale Donald. *Conversations with God: An Uncommon Dialogue, Book 1*. New York: Putnam, 1996.

Tourette Syndrome

Mayo Clinic. "Tourette Syndrome." Retrieved October 3, 2020, from https://www.mayoclinic.org/diseases-conditions/tourette-syndrome/symptoms-causes/syc-20350465.

Tourette Association of America. https://tourette.org.

About the Author

After the death of her sixteen-year-old son Collin, Susan Glynn Robinson found herself trapped in deep, debilitating grief. Family and friends created a loving, supportive cushion as she struggled to find a way through the despair. Writing this story helped her come to terms with her self-image, manage raging emotions, and search for answers to existential questions. She hopes her experience will smooth the way for others wrestling their own grief monsters.

A former classroom teacher and college writing instructor, Susan's passions are reading, writing, and teaching—and her grandkids. Her perfect day includes relaxing on the beach and reading with her sweeties.

Susan lives with her husband, Ed, and their Aussie, Bailey. She is the author of children's picture books *When Poke Woke* and *Poke's Toque*.

Thank you for reading *Say His Name: A Mother's Grief.*
I hope my story resonated with you and that you discovered a few
nuggets of wisdom to guide you through your grief.

I welcome your feedback. Write to me at
Susan@SusanRobinsonAuthor.com.

Be the first to learn of new releases,
blog posts, events, and freebies.

Like SusanRobinsonAuthor on Facebook.

Visit my webpage and sign up for my email list at
https://www.susanrobinsonauthor.com.